Cyrus Hall McCormick

Also from Westphalia Press
westphaliapress.org

Cyrus Hall McCormick

His Life and Work

by Herbert N. Casson

WESTPHALIA PRESS
An Imprint of Policy Studies Organization

Cyrus Hall McCormick: His Life and Work
All Rights Reserved © 2017 by Policy Studies Organization

Westphalia Press
An imprint of Policy Studies Organization
1527 New Hampshire Ave., NW
Washington, D.C. 20036
info@ipsonet.org

ISBN-13: 978-1-63391-542-8
ISBN-10: 1-63391-542-5

Cover design by Jeffrey Barnes:
jbarnesbook.design

Daniel Gutierrez-Sandoval, Executive Director
PSO and Westphalia Press

Updated material and comments on this edition
can be found at the Westphalia Press website:
www.westphaliapress.org

CYRUS HALL McCORMICK
HIS LIFE AND WORK

C. H. McCormick

The Lakeside Press
R. R. DONNELLEY & SONS COMPANY
CHICAGO

CYRUS HALL McCORMICK

HIS LIFE AND WORK

BY

HERBERT N. CASSON

AUTHOR OF
" THE ROMANCE OF STEEL," " THE ROMANCE OF THE REAPER," ETC.

ILLUSTRATED

CHICAGO
A. C. McCLURG & CO.
1909

INTRODUCTION

WHOEVER wishes to understand the making of the United States must read the life of Cyrus Hall McCormick. No other one man so truly represented the dawn of the industrial era,— the grapple of the pioneer with the crudities of a new country, the replacing of muscle with machinery, and the establishment of better ways and better times in farm and city alike. Beginning exactly one hundred years ago, the life of McCormick spanned the heroic period of our industrial advancement, when great things were done by great individuals. To know McCormick is to know what type of man it was who created the United States of the nineteenth century. And now that a new century has arrived, with a new type of business development, it may be especially instructive to review a life that was so structural and so fundamental.

As Professor Simon Newcomb has observed, "It is impressive to think how few men we should have had to remove from the earth during the past three centuries to have stopped the advance of our civilization." From this point of view, there are few, if any, who will appear to be more indispensable than McCormick. He was not brilliant. He was not picturesque. He was no caterer for fame or favor. But he was as necessary as bread. He fed his country as truly as Washington created it and Lincoln preserved it. He abolished our agricultural peasantry so effectively that we have had to import our muscle from foreign countries ever since. And he added an immense province to the new empire of mind over matter, the expansion of which has been and is now the highest and most important of all human endeavors.

As the master builder of the modern business of manufacturing farm machinery, McCormick set in motion so many forces of human betterment that the fruitfulness of his life can never be fully told. There are to-day in all countries more than one hundred thousand patents for inventions that were meant to lighten the labor of the farmer. And the cereal crop of the world has risen with incredible gains, until this year its value will be not far from ten thousand millions of dollars,— very nearly the equivalent of all the gold in coin and jewelry and bullion.

So, if there is not power and fascination in this story, it will be the fault of the story-teller, and not of his theme. The story itself is destined to be told and retold. It cannot be forgotten, because it is one of those rare life-histories that blazon out the peculiar genius of the nation under the stress of a new experience. As it is passed on from generation to generation, it may finally be polished into an Epic of the Wheat,— the tale of Man's long wrestle with Famine, and how he won at last by creating a world-wide system for the production and distribution of the Bread.

H. N. C.

Chicago, *September 1, 1909.*

CONTENTS

ILLUSTRATIONS

ILLUSTRATIONS

CYRUS HALL McCORMICK
HIS LIFE AND WORK

CHAPTER I

THE WORLD'S NEED OF A REAPER

EITHER by a very strange coincidence, or as a phenomenon of the instinct of self-preservation, the year 1809, which was marked by famine and tragedy in almost every quarter of the globe, was also a most prolific birthyear for men of genius. Into this year came Poe, Blackie, and Tennyson, the poet laureates of America, Scotland, and England; Chopin and Mendelssohn, the apostles of sweeter music; Lincoln, who kept the United States united; Baron Haussemann, the beautifier of Paris; Proudhon, the prophet of communism; Lord Houghton, who did much in science, and Darwin, who did most; FitzGerald, who made known the literature of Persia; Bonar, who wrote hymns; Kinglake, who wrote histories; Holmes, who

wrote sentiment and humor; Gladstone, who
ennobled the politics of the British empire; and
McCormick, who gave the world cheap bread,
and whose life-story is now set before us in the
following pages.

None of these eminent men, except Lincoln,
began life in as remote and secluded a corner of
the world as McCormick. His father's farm
was at the northern edge of Rockbridge County,
Virginia, in a long, thin strip of fairly fertile land
that lay crumpled between the Blue Ridge on
the east and the Alleghanies on the west. It
was eighteen miles south of the nearest town of
Staunton, and a hundred miles from the Atlantic
coast. The whole region was a quiet, industrious
valley, whose only local tragedy had been an
Indian massacre in 1764, in which eighty white
settlers had been put to death by a horde of
savages.

The older men and women of 1809 could
remember when wolf-heads were used as currency; and when the stocks and the ducking-
stool stood in the main street of Staunton. Also,
they were fond of telling how the farmers of the

valley, when they heard that the Revolution had begun in Massachusetts, carted 137 barrels of flour to Frederick, one hundred miles north, and ordered it sent forthwith to the needy people of Boston. This grew to be one of the most popular tales of local history,— an epic of the patriots who fought for liberty, not with gunpowder but flour.

By 1809 the more severe hardships of the pioneer days had been overcome. Houses were still built of logs, but they were larger and better furnished. In the McCormick homestead, for instance, there was a parlor which had the dignity of mahogany furniture, and the luxury of books and a carpet. The next-door county of Augusta boasted of thirteen carriages and one hundred and two cut-glass decanters. And the chief sources of excitement had evolved from Indian raids and wolf-hunts into elections, lotteries, and litigation.

It was perhaps fortunate for the child McCormick that he was born in such an out-of-the-way nook, for the reason that in 1809 almost the whole civilized world was in a turmoil. In England mobs of unemployed men and women were either begging for bread or smashing the new machines that had displaced them in the factories. In the Tyrol, sixty thousand peasants, who had revolted from the intolerable tyranny of the Bavarians, were being beaten into submission. In Servia, the Turks were striking down a rebellion by building a pyramid of thirty thousand Servian skulls,— a tragic pile which may still be seen midway between Belgrade and Stamboul. Sweden was being trampled under the feet of a Russian army; and the greater part of Holland, Austria, Germany, and Spain had been so scourged by the hosts of Napoleon as to be one vast shamble of misery and blood.

In the United States there was no war, but there certainly did exist an abnormal surplus of adversity. The young republic, which had fewer white citizens than the two cities of New York and Chicago possess to-day, was being terrorized in the West by the Indian Confederacy of Tecumseh; and its flag had been flouted by England, France, and the Barbary pirates. Its total revenue was much less than the value of

last year's hay crop in Vermont.   It was desper-
ately poor, with its people housed for the most
part in log cabins, clothed in homespun, and fed
every winter on food that would cause a riot in
any modern penitentiary.

There was no such thing known, except in
dreams, as the use of machinery in the cultivation of the soil.   The average farmer, in all
civilized countries, believed that an iron plow
would poison the soil.   He planted his grain by
the phases of the moon; kept his cows outside in
winter; and was unaware that glanders was contagious.   Joseph Jenks, of Lynn, had invented
the scythe in 1655, "for the more speedy cutting
of grasse"; and a Scotchman had improved it
into the grain cradle.   But the greater part of
the grain in all countries was, a century ago,
being cut by the same little hand sickle that the
Egyptians had used on the banks of the Nile
and the Babylonians in the valley of the Euphrates.

The wise public men of that day knew how
urgent was the need of better methods in farming.   Fifteen years before, George Washington

had said, "I know of no pursuit in which more real and important service can be rendered to any country than by improving its agriculture." But it was generally believed that the task was hopeless; and any effort to encourage inventors had hitherto been a failure.   An English society, for instance, had offered a prize of one hundred and fifty dollars for a better method of reaping grain, and the only answer it received was from a traveller who had seen the Belgians reaping with a two-foot scythe and a cane; the cane was used to push the grain back before it was cut, so that more grain could be cut at a blow. As to whether or not he received the prize for this discovery is not recorded.

The city of New York in 1809 was not larger than the Des Moines of to-day, and not nearly so well built and prosperous.   Two miles to the north of it, through swamps and forests, lay the clearing that is now known as Herald Square. There was no street railway, nor cooking range, nor petroleum, nor savings bank, nor friction match, nor steel plow, neither in New York nor anywhere else.   And the one pride and boast of the city was Fulton's new steamboat, the *Clermont*, which could waddle to Albany and back, if all went well, in three days or possibly four.

As for social conditions, they were so hopelessly bad that few had the heart to improve them. The house that we call a "slum tenement" to-day would have made an average American hotel in 1809. Rudeness and rowdyism were the rule. Drunkenness was as common, and as little considered, as smoking is at the present time; there was no organized opposition to it of any kind, except one little temperance society at Saratoga. There were no sewers, and much of the water was drawn from putrid wells. Many faces were pitted with small-pox. Cholera and yellow jack or strange hunger-fevers cut wide swaths of death again and again among the helpless people. There was no science, of course, and no sanitation, and no medical knowledge except a medley of drastic measures which were apt to be as dangerous as the disease.

The desperate struggle to survive appears

to have been so intense that there was little or
no social sympathy.   There was very little
pity for the pauper,— he was auctioned off to
be half starved by the lowest bidder; and for
the criminal there was no feeling except the
utmost repulsion and abhorrence. It was
found, for instance, in 1809, that in the jail
in New York there were seventy-two women,
white and black, in one chairless, bedless room,
all kept in order by a keeper with a whip, and
fed like cattle from a tub of mush, some eating
with spoons and some with cups and some with
their unwashed hands.   And the men's room
of that jail, says this report, "is worse than the
women's."

Also, in 1809, the chronic quantity of misery
had been terribly augmented by the Embargo,
— that most ruinous invention of President
Jefferson, whereby American ships were swept
from the sea, with a loss to capital of twelve
millions a year, and a loss to labor of thirty
thousand places of employment. According
to this amazing act of political folly, every
market-boat sailing from New Jersey to New

York — every sailboat or canoe — had to give bail to the federal government before it dared to leave the dock.

Whatever flimsy little structure of industry had been built up in thirty years of independence, was thrown prostrate by this Embargo. A hundred thousand men stood on the streets with helpless hands, begging for work or bread. The jails were jammed with debtors,— 1,300 in New York alone. The newspapers were overrun by bankruptcy notices. The coffee-houses were empty. The ships lay mouldering at the docks. In those hand-to-mouth days there was no piled-up reserve of food or wealth, — no range of towering wheat-banks at every port; and the seaboard cities lay for a time as desolate as though they had been ravaged by a pestilence.

In that darkest year the hardscrabble little republic learned and remembered one of its most important lessons,— the fact that liberty and independence are not enough. Here it was, an absolutely free nation,— *the only free civilized country in the world*,— and yet as miserable and poor and hungry as though it were a mere province of a European empire. So, by degrees, there came a change in the American point of view,— a swing from politicalism to industrialism. The mass of the people were now surfeited with oratory and politics and war. They began to settle down to hard facts and hard work. Instead of declaiming about the rights of man, they began to build roads and weave cloth and organize stock companies. Slowly they came to realize that a second Revolution must be wrought,— a Revolution that would enable them to write a Declaration of Independence against Hunger and Hardship and Hand Labor.

Up to the year 1809 the chief topics of interest in American legislatures and grocery stores were the blockades, the Embargo, the treaties, the badness of Napoleon, the blunders of Jefferson, and the rudeness of England and France. But after that year the chief topics of interest came to be of a wholly different sort. They were such as the tariff, the currency, the building of factories and canals, the opening of public lands, the problem of slavery, and the development of the West. The hardy, victorious little nation began to talk less and work more; and so by a natural evolution of thought the era of George Washington and Thomas Jefferson came to an end, and the era of Robert Fulton and Peter Cooper and Cyrus Hall McCormick was in its dawn.

From 1810 to 1820 there was a rush to the land. Twenty million acres were sold, in most cases for two dollars an acre. Thousands of men who had been sailors turned their backs on the sea and learned to till the soil. Town laborers, too, whose wages had been fifty cents a day, tramped westward along the Indian trails and seized upon scraps of land that lay ownerless. Nine out of ten Americans began to farm with the utmost energy and perseverance,— *but with what tools?* With the wooden plow, the sickle, the scythe, and the flail, the same rude hand-labor tools that the nations of antiquity had tried to farm with,— the tools of failure and slavery and famine.

Such was the predicament of this republic

for the first seventy-five years of its life. It could not develop beyond the struggle for food. It was chained to the bread-line. It could not feed itself. Not even nine-tenths of its people could produce enough grain to satisfy its hunger. Again and again, until 1858, wheat had to be imported by this nation of farmers. So, as we now look back over those basic years, from the summit of the twentieth century, we can see how timely an event it was that in the dark year 1809 the inventor of the Reaper was born.

CHAPTER II

THE McCORMICK HOME

IF we wish to solve the riddle of the Reaper, — to know why it was not invented in any of the older nations that rose to greatness and perished in so many instances for lack of bread, — we can find the key to the answer in the home and the ancestry of the McCormicks. We shall see that the family into which he was born represented in the highest degree that new species of farmer,— self-reliant, studious, enterprising, and inventive,— which was developed in the pioneer period of American history.

Robert McCormick, the father of Cyrus, was in his most prosperous days the owner of four farms, having in all 1,800 acres. But his acres were only one-half of his interests. He owned as well two grist-mills, two sawmills, a smelting-furnace, a distillery, and a blacksmith-shop. He did much more than till the soil. He hammered iron and shaped wood, and did both well, as those can testify who have seen an iron crane and walnut cabinet that were made by his hands. More than this, he invented new types of farm machinery,— a hemp-brake, a clover huller, a bellows, and a threshing-machine.

The little log workshop still stands where Robert McCormick and his sons hammered and tinkered on rainy days. It is about twenty-four feet square, with an uneven floor, and a heavy door that was hung in place by home-made nails and home-made hinges. There was a forge on either side of the chimney, so that two men could work at the same time; and one small rusted anvil is all that now remains of its equipment.

As for the McCormick homestead itself, there were so many manufacturing activities in it that it was literally half a home and half a factory. Shoes were cobbled, cotton, flax, and wool were spun into yarn, woven into cloth, and fashioned into clothes for the whole family. The stockings and mitts and caps were all home-made, and so was the cradle in which the eight children were rocked. What with the moulding of candles, and sewing of carpet-rags, and curing of hams,

OLD BLACKSMITH SHOP ON WALNUT GROVE FARM, VIRGINIA

In this shop the first practical reaping machine was built by Cyrus Hall McCormick in 1831

and boiling of soap, and drying of herbs, and stringing of apples, the McCormick home was practically a school of many trades for the people who lived under its roof.

Robert McCormick was an educated man. He was not at all like the poor serfs who tilled the soil of Europe. He belonged to the same general class as those other eminent farmers,— Washington, Jefferson, Adams, Webster, and Clay. He was a reader of deep books and a student of astronomy. Lawyers and clergymen would frequently drive to his house to consult with him. And in mechanical pursuits he had an unusual degree of skill, having been born the son of a weaver and accustomed from babyhood to the use of machinery.

He was a gentle, reflective man, with a genius for self-reliance in any great or little emergency. When a new stone church was built, and he found that his pew was so dark that he could not see to read the hymns, he promptly cut a small window in the wall,— a peculiarity which is still pointed out to visitors. On another occasion, with this same spirit of resourcefulness, he drove the spectre of yellow fever from the home. This dreaded disease was gathering in a full harvest in the farm-houses of the county. It had cut down three of Mrs. McCormick's family,— her father, mother, and brother, — and had swung its fatal scythe toward the boy Cyrus, who was then five years of age. When the doctor was called, he insisted that the child should be bled. "But you bled all the others, and they died," said Robert McCormick quietly; "I 'll have no more bleedings." No remedy for yellow fever, except bleeding, was known to the doctors of a century ago, so Robert McCormick at once invented a remedy. He devised a treatment of hot baths, hot teas, and bitter herbs; and Cyrus was rescued from the fever and restored to perfect health.

Such a man as Robert McCormick would have been practically impossible in any other country at that time. There, in that isolated hollow of the Virginian mountains, he was a citizen of a free country. His vote had helped to make Thomas Jefferson President. He was a proprietor, not a serf nor a tenant. He was not compelled to divide up every cord of wood and bushel of wheat with a king or a landlord. Whatever he earned was his own. He was an American; and thus, in the endless chain of cause and effect, we can trace the origin of the Reaper back, if we wish, to George Washington and Christopher Columbus.

The whole spirit of the young republic pushed towards the invention of labor-saving machinery, — towards replacing the hoe with the steel plow, the needle with the sewing-machine, the puddling-furnace with the Bessemer converter, the sickle with the Reaper. And it is fair to say that the social forces that represented the American spirit were focused to a remarkable degree in the home in which Cyrus H. McCormick had his birth and his education.

There was another contributing influence, too, in the making of McCormick,— the fact that the blood of his father and mother came to him in a pure strain of Scotch-Irish. It was this inheritance that endowed him with the tenacity and unconquerable resiliency that enabled him not only to invent a new machine, but to create a new industry and hold fast to it against all comers.

The Scotch-Irish! The full story of what the United States owes to this fire-hardened race has never yet been told, — it is a tale that will some day be expanded into a fascinating volume of American history. It is not possible to understand either the character or the success of McCormick without knowing the Scotch-Irish influences that shaped him.

The one man who did more to launch the Scotch-Irish on their conquering way, so it appears, was John Knox. This preacher-statesman, "who never feared the face of man," forced Queen Mary from her throne, and established self-government and a pure religion in Scotland, about seventy-five years after the discovery of America. This brought English armies down upon the Scotch, and for very nearly two centuries the struggle was bitter and desperate, the Scotch refusing to compromise or to bate one jot or tittle of a covenant which many of them had signed with their blood.

At the height of this conflict, about 300,000

THE OLD McCORMICK HOMESTEAD, WALNUT GROVE FARM, ROCKBRIDGE COUNTY, VIRGINIA

of these Scotch Covenanters left their ravaged
country and set out in a fleet of little vessels for
the north of Ireland. Here they settled in the
barren and boggy province of Ulster, and presto!
in the course of two generations Ulster became
the most prosperous, moral, and intelligent section of the British empire. Its people were,
beyond a doubt, the best educated masses of
that period, either in Great Britain or anywhere
else. They were the most skilful of farmers.
They wove woollen cloth and the finest of linen.
They built schools and churches and factories.
But in 1698, the English Parliament, jealous of
such progressiveness, passed laws against their
manufacturing, and Ulster was overrun, as
Scotland had been, with the police and the
soldiery of England.

The Scotch-Irish fought, of course, even
against such odds. They had never learned
how to submit. But as the devastation of Ulster
continued, they resolved to do as their great-
grandfathers had done, — emigrate to a new
country. They had heard good reports of America, through several of their leaders who had

been banished there by the British government. So they packed up their movable property, and set out across the wide uncharted Atlantic Ocean in an exodus for liberty of industry and liberty of conscience.

By the year 1776 there were more than 500,000 of the Scotch-Irish in this country. They went first across the Alleghanies, into the new lands of western Virginia, Tennessee, Kentucky, and Texas. Beyond all question, they were the hardiest and ablest founders of the republic. They dissolved the rule of the Cavaliers in Virginia; and in the little hamlet of Mecklenburg they planned the first defiance of Great Britain and struck the key-note of the Revolution. They gave Washington thirty-nine of his generals, three out of four members of his cabinet, and three out of five judges of the first Supreme Court.

Of all classes of settlers in the thirteen colonies, they were the best prepared and most willing for the struggle with England, for the reason that they had begun to fight for liberty two hundred and fifty years before the battle of

Bunker Hill. They were not amateurs in the work of revolution. They were veterans. And so, because they were pioneers and patriots by nature and inheritance, the Scotch-Irish became, in the words of John Fiske, "the main strength of our American democracy."

Naturally, they were pathfinders in industry as well as in the matter of self-government, as many of them had been manufacturers in Ireland. "Thousands of the best manufacturers and weavers in Ulster went to seek their bread in America," writes Froude, "and they carried their art and their tools with them." In one instance, by the failure of the woollen trade, 20,000 of them were driven to the United States. As might have been expected, these Scotch-Irish Americans have produced not only five of our Presidents, but also such merchants as A. T. Stewart; such publishers as Harper, Bonner, Scribner, and McClurg; and such inventors as Joseph Henry, Morse, Fulton, and McCormick. They were possibly the first large body of people who had ever been driven from manufacturing into farming; and it was not at all surprising, therefore, that the new profession of making farm machinery should have been born upon a Scotch-Irish farm.

As for Cyrus H. McCormick, he represented the fourth generation of American McCormicks. His great-grandfather, Thomas McCormick, quit Ulster in the troublous days of 1735. He was a soldier at Londonderry; and later became noted as an Indian fighter in Pennsylvania. His son Robert, who moved south to Virginia, carried a rifle for American independence at the battle of Guilford Court-house, North Carolina, in 1781. He was a farmer and weaver by occupation, a typical Ulsterman, whose farm was a busy workshop of invention and manufacturing.

On his mother's side, too, Cyrus McCormick had behind him a line of battling Scotch-Irish. She was the daughter of a Virginian farmer named Patrick Hall, one of whose forefathers had been driven out of Armagh by the massacre of 1641. Patrick Hall was the leader of the old-school Presbyterians in his region of Virginia. So rigid was he in his loyalty to the faith of the

ROBERT McCORMICK

Covenanters, that once when a new minister came to preach in the little kirk, and lined out a Watts hymn instead of a psalm of David, Patrick Hall picked up his hat and strode out, followed by a goodly part of the congregation. He at once built upon his own farm a new church of limestone, in which no such levity as hymn-singing was permitted.

Cyrus McCormick's mother inherited her father's strength of character, without his severity. She was a thorough Celt, impulsive, free-spoken, and highly imaginative. Judging from the stories about her that are remembered in the neighborhood, it is evident that she was a woman of exceptional quality of mind. She was not as studious as her husband, but quicker and more ambitious. As a girl, she had been strikingly handsome, with a tall and commanding figure. She was saving and shrewd, with the Scotch-Irish passion for "getting ahead." She allowed no idle moments in the home. If the children were dressed before breakfast was ready, out they went to cut wood or weed the garden. She knew the profession

of housekeeping in all its old-fashioned com-
plexity; and she worked at it from dawn to
starlight, with no rest except the relief of flitting
from one task to another.

"Mrs. McCormick came riding by our farm
one day," said an aged neighbor, "at a time
when my father and mother were hurrying to
save some hay from a coming rain-storm. 'If
you don't hurry up you 'll be too late,' she said;
and then tying her horse to the fence she picked
up a rake and helped with the hay until it was
all in the barn. That 's the kind of woman she
was,— always full of energy and ready to help."

But Mrs. McCormick was much more than
industrious. She had a fine pride in the owner-
ship of beautiful things,— flowers and handsome clothes and silverware and mahogany
furniture. Her flock of peacocks was one of
the sights of the county; and in her later life,
when she was for ten years the sole manager of
the farm, she was accustomed to drive about in
a wonderful carriage with folding steps, drawn
by prancing horses and driven by a stately col-
ored coachman,— an equipage of so much

MRS. MARY ANN HALL McCORMICK

style and grandeur that it is still remembered by the neighbors. "She loved to drive fast," said one old lady; "and I was much impressed as a little girl with the startling way in which her horses would come clattering and dancing up to the door."

Thus there was in the McCormick home the spiritual and imaginative element that was vital to the development of a man whose whole life was a battle against the prejudices and "impossibilities" of the world. Cyrus McCormick was predestined, we may legitimately say, by the conditions of his birth, to accomplish his great work. From his father he had a specific training as an inventor; from his mother he had executive ability and ambition; from his Scotch-Irish ancestry he had the dogged tenacity that defied defeat; and from the wheat-fields that environed his home came the call for the Reaper, to lighten the heavy drudgery of the harvest.

CHAPTER III

THE INVENTION OF THE REAPER

NOT far from the McCormick homestead was the "Old Field School," built of logs and with a part of one of the upper logs cut out to provide a window. Here the boy Cyrus sat on a slab bench and studied five books as though they were the only books in the world,— Murray's Grammar, Dilworth's Arithmetic, Webster's Spelling Book, the Shorter Catechism, and the Bible.

He was a strong-limbed, self-contained, serious-natured boy, always profoundly intent upon what he was doing. Even at the age of fifteen he was inventive. One winter morning he brought to school a most elaborate map of the world, showing the two hemispheres side by side. First he had drawn it in ink upon paper, then pasted the paper upon linen, and hung it upon two varnished rollers. This map, which is still preserved, reveals a remarkable degree of skill and patience; and the fact that a mere lad could conceive of and create such a map was a week's wonder in the little community. "That boy," declared the teacher, "is beyond me."

At about this time he undertook to do a man's work in the reaping of the wheat, and here he discovered that to swing a cradle against a field of grain under a hot summer sun was of all farming drudgeries the severest. Both his back and his brain rebelled against it. One thing at least he could do,— he could make a smaller cradle, that would be easier to swing; and he did this, whittling away in the evening in the little log workshop.

"Cyrus was a natural mechanical genius," said an old laborer who had worked on the McCormick farm. "He was always trying to invent something." "He was a young man of great and superior talents," said a neighbor. At eighteen he studied the profession of surveying, and made a quadrant for his own use. This is still preserved, and bears witness to his good workmanship. From this time until his twenty-second year, there is nothing of exceptional interest recorded of him. He had grown to be

a tall, muscular, dignified young man. The
neighbors, in later years, remembered him
mainly because he was so well dressed on
Sundays, in broadcloth coat and beaver hat,
and because of his fine treble voice as he led
the singing in the country church.

Even as a youth he was absorbed in his inventions and business projects. He had no time
for gayeties. In a letter written from Kentucky
to a cousin, Adam McChesney, in 1831, he says:
"Mr. Hart has two fine daughters, right pretty,
very smart, and as rich probably as you would
wish; but alas! I have other business to attend
to."

Ever since Cyrus was a child of seven, it
had been the most ardent ambition of his father
to invent a Reaper. He had made one and
tried it in the harvest of 1816, but it was a failure.
It was a fantastic machine, pushed from behind
by two horses. A row of short curved sickles
were fastened to upright posts, and the grain
was whirled against them by revolving rods.
It was highly ingenious, but the sinewy grain
merely bunched and tangled around its futile

NEW PROVIDENCE CHURCH, ROCKBRIDGE COUNTY, VIRGINIA

sickles; and the poor old Reaper that would not reap was hauled off the field, to become one of the jokes of the neighborhood.

This failure did not dishearten Robert McCormick. He persevered with Scotch-Irish tenacity, but in secret. Hurt by the jests of the neighbors, he worked thenceforward with the door of his workshop locked, or at night. He hid his Reaper, too, upon a shelf inside the workshop. "He allowed no one to see what he was doing, except his sons," said Davis McCormick, who is now the only living person in the neighborhood with a memory that extends back to that early period. "Yes," said this lone octogenarian, "Robert McCormick was a good man, a true Christian; and he worked for years to make a Reaper. He always kept his plans to himself, and he told his wife that if visitors came to the house, she should send one of the children to fetch him, and not allow the visitors to come to his workshop."

By the early Summer of 1831, Robert McCormick had so improved his Reaper that he gave it a trial in a field of grain. Again it was a failure. It did cut the grain fairly well, but flung it in a tangled heap. As much as this had been done before by other machines, and it was not enough. To cut the grain was only one-half of the problem; the other half of the problem, which up to this time no one had solved, was how to properly handle and deliver the grain after it was cut.

By this time Cyrus had become as much of a Reaper enthusiast as his father. Also, he had been studying out the reasons for his father's failure, and working out in his mind a new plan of construction. How this *new plan* was slowly moulded into shape by his creative fancy is now told for the first time. A manuscript, written by Cyrus H. McCormick himself, and which has not hitherto been made public, gives a complete description of the process of thought by which he became the inventor of the first practical Reaper. This account, it may be said in explanation, was written by Mr. McCormick shortly before the Chicago fire of 1871. It was to be published at that time, and was in type when the fire came and left not a vestige

At the commencement of the harvest of ~~At~~

Robt.

~~In~~ 1831, Mr. McCormick, ~~father~~ ~~&~~

made another trial of his ~~neighbor~~

~~if practical~~

again without success, and when, being satisfied

that his principle of operating ~~was~~

~~laid aside and~~

~~who had been witnessing his father's experiments~~

his son, then perceiving the difficulty

himself

in the way of his father's success, ~~while~~

never having seen, or heard of any other

experiment or principles ~~of person~~ but

his father's in connection with grain reaping

by ~~horse~~ power, devoted himself to most

laborionsly to the discovery of a principle

of operating upon which to carry out the

~~for~~

great object, which his father had labored

both mentally and physically for fifteen

years.   as his father also had found,

Finding, that the difficulty of separating

the grain to be cut between each two of the

"cylinders" ~~referred to~~, when in a fallen or tangled

state, was insurmountable; and that, therefore,

to succeed, the grain must be cut without such

separation, except at the line of division be-

tween the swath to be cut and the grain

to be left standing, ~~which the obvious~~ point

the ~~ascertained~~ difficulty had to be overcome

this question first to be solved was how that

was possible. ~~can be done~~   In his reflecting &

reasoning on this point it occurred to him that

to effect the cutting of the grain by a cutting

2³

instrument, that through a certain amount of motion that was necessary—this was indeed demonstrated by the cutters on the grain of the ~~scissors~~ cradle then in common use. The next thought was that while the motion forward as drawn by horses was not sufficient, a lateral motion must at the same time be communicated to the cutting instrument, which, combined with the forward motion, would be sufficient to effect the cutting process as the machine advanced upon the grain. How then was this to be effected?

Two different methods occured to the mind of the inventor before he undertook to put either to the test of trial in the field: One was that of a revolving wheel placed horizontally (as the wheel of a cart), and drawn forward which caused to revolve rapidly on its axis the grain having a cutting edge placed on its periphery. Not satisfied, however, with this idea — many objecting & difficulties in way of its success presenting themselves to the mind of Mr McCormick — his next thought the idea which proved to be the foundation upon which his great invention was finally based was that their placing of a straight cutting blade by of communicating the requisite lateral motion to a straight cutting blade, placed at right angles to the line of draught of the machine. This first principle he immediately

Left margin: Brown's (?)

HIS OWN ACCOUNT OF THE ORIGIN OF THE REAPER

of the printery. The original manuscript was
preserved; but the labor of rebuilding his factory prevented him from carrying out his original
design. He wholly forgot his authorship in the
troubles of his city; and so his own story of his
invention lay untouched among the private
papers of the family for thirty-eight years.

"Robert McCormick," says this document,
"being satisfied that his principle of operation
could not succeed, laid aside and abandoned the
further prosecution of his idea." He had
labored for fifteen years to make a Reaper that
would reap, and he had failed.

At this point Cyrus took up the work that
his father had reluctantly abandoned. He had
never seen or heard of any Reaper experiments
except those of his father; but he believed he saw
a better way, and "devoted himself most laboriously to the discovery of a *new principle of
operation.*"

He showed his originality at the outset by
beginning where his father and all other Reaper
inventors had left off,— with the cutting of grain
that lay in a fallen and tangled mass. He faced

the problem worst end first. The Reaper that would cut such grain, he believed, must first separate the grain that is to be cut from the grain that is left standing. It must have at the end of its knife a curved arm — a *divider*. This idea was simple, but in the long history of harvesting grain no one had thought of it before.

Next, in order to cut this snarled and prostrate grain without missing any of it, the knife must have two motions: its forward motion, as drawn by the horses, and also a slashing sideways motion of its own. How was this to be done? McCormick's first thought was to cut the grain with a whirling wheel-knife, but this plan presented too many new difficulties. Suddenly the idea came to him — why not have a straight blade, with a back and forward motion of its own? This was the birth-idea of the *reciprocating blade*, which has been used to this day on all grain-cutting machines. It was not, like the divider, a wholly new conception; but Cyrus McCormick conceived it independently, and did more than any one else to establish it as the basic feature of the Reaper.

The third problem was the supporting of the grain while it was being cut, so that the knife would not merely flatten it to the ground.   Mc-Cormick solved this by placing a row of *fingers* at the edge of the blade.   These fingers projected a few inches, in such a way that the grain was caught and held in position to be cut.   The shape of these fingers was afterwards much improved, to prevent wet grain from clogging the slit in which the knife slid back and forth.

A fourth device was still needed to lift up and straighten the grain that had fallen.   This was done by a simple revolving *reel*, such as fishermen use for the drying of their nets.   Several of the abortive Reapers that had been tried elsewhere had possessed some sort of a reel; but McCormick made his much larger than any other, so that no grain was too low to escape it.

The fifth factor in this assembling of a Reaper was the *platform*, to catch the cut grain as it fell; and from which the grain was to be raked off by a man who walked alongside of it.   The sixth was the idea of putting the shafts on the outside, or stubble side, of the Reaper, making it a *side-*

draught, instead of a "push" machine. And the seventh and final factor was the building of the whole Reaper upon one big *driving-wheel*, which carried the weight and operated the reel and cutting-blade. The grain-side end of the blade was at first supported by a wooden runner, and later — the following year — by a small wheel.

Such was the making of the first practical Reaper in the history of the world. It was as clumsy as a Red River ox-cart; but *it reaped*. It was made on right lines. The "new principle" that the youth McCormick laboriously conceived in the little log workshop became the basic type of a wholly new machine. It has never been displaced. Since then there have been 12,000 patents issued for reaper and mower inventions; but not one of them has overthrown the type of the first McCormick Reaper. Not one of the seven factors that he assembled has been thrown aside; and the most elaborate self-binder of to-day is a direct descendant of the crude machine that was thus created by a young Virginian farmer in 1831.

FIRST PRACTICAL REAPING MACHINE

Built and used by Cyrus Hall McCormick on Walnut Grove Farm, Va., in 1831

The young inventor toiled "laboriously," he says, to complete his Reaper in time for the harvest of 1831. He was very nearly too late, but a small patch of wheat was left standing at his request; and one day in July, with no spectators except his parents and his excited brothers and sisters, Cyrus put a horse between the shafts of his Reaper, and drove against the yellow grain. The reel revolved and swept the gentle wheat downwards upon the knife. Click! Click! Click! The white steel blade shot back and forth. The grain was cut. It fell upon the platform in a shimmering golden swath. From here it was raked off by a young laborer named John Cash. It was a roughly done specimen of reaping, no doubt. The reel and the divider worked poorly. But for a preliminary test it was a magnificent success. Here, at last, was a Reaper that reaped, the first that had ever been made in any country.

The scene of this first "reaping by horse-power" was then, and is to-day, one of unusual beauty. The field is near by the farm-house, rolling in several undulations to the rim of a

winding little rivulet. In the centre of the field
is a single tree, a wide-branched white oak,
which was probably born before the first col-
onists arrived at Jamestown. And in the back-
ground, not more than two miles distant, rise the
tall and jagged crags of the Blue Ridge, twelve
sharp peaks flung high from deep ravines, on
which the lights and shades are incessantly
changing,— a most impressive staging for the
first act of the drama of the Reaper.

This McCormick farm, having 600 acres of
land, is now owned by the McCormick family.
The whole region has changed but little. Once,
and once only, the great noisy outside world
surged into this quiet valley,— when a Union
army under General Butler clattered through it,
burning and destroying, and so close to the Mc-
Cormick homestead that the blue uniforms could
be seen from its front windows. Doubtless,
when farmers have time to take a proper pride
in the history of their own profession, they will
visit the McCormick farm as a spot of historic
interest,— the place where the New Argicul-
ture was born. It is no longer a difficult place

to reach, as it is now possible to lunch to-day in either Chicago or New York and to-morrow in the same comfortable red brick farm-house that sheltered the McCormicks in 1831.

Several days after the advent of the Reaper on the home farm, Cyrus McCormick had improved its reel and divider, and was ready for a public exhibition at the near-by village of Steele's Tavern. Here, with two horses, he cut six acres of oats in an afternoon, a feat which was attested in court in 1848 by his brothers William and Leander, and also by three of the villagers, John Steele, Eliza Steele, and Dr. N. M. Hitt. Such a thing at that time was incredible. It was equal to the work of six laborers with scythes, or twenty-four peasants with sickles. It was as marvellous as though a man should walk down the street carrying a dray-horse on his back.

The next year, 1832, Cyrus McCormick came out with his Reaper into what seemed to him "the wide, wide world." He gave a public exhibition near the little town of Lexington, which lay eighteen miles south of the farm. Fully one

[37]

hundred people were present — several political leaders of local fame, farmers, professors,
laborers, and a group of negroes who frolicked
and shouted in uncomprehending joy.

At the start, it appeared as though this new
contraption of a machine, which was unlike anything else that human eyes had ever seen, was
to prove a grotesque failure. The field was
hilly, and the Reaper jolted and slewed so vio-
lently that John Ruff, the owner of the field,
made a loud protest.

"Here! This won't do," he shouted. "Stop
your horses. You are rattling the heads off my
wheat."

This was a hard blow to the young farmer-
inventor. Several laborers, who were openly
hostile to the machine as their rival in the labor
market, began to jeer with great satisfaction.
"It's a humbug," said one. "Give me the old
cradle yet, boys," said another. These men
were hardened and bent and calloused with the
drudgery of harvesting. They worked twelve
and fourteen hours a day for less than a nickel
an hour. But they were as resentful toward

THE FIELD ON WHICH THE FIRST McCORMICK REAPER WAS TRIED, WALNUT GROVE FARM, VIRGINIA

a Reaper as the drivers of stage-coaches were to railroads, or as the hackmen of to-day are towards automobiles.

At this moment of apparent defeat, a man of striking appearance, who had been watching the floundering of the Reaper with great interest, came to the rescue.

"I'll give you a fair chance, young man," he said. "That field of wheat on the other side of the fence belongs to me. Pull down the fence and cross over."

This friend in need was the Honorable William Taylor, who was several years later a candidate for the governorship of Virginia. His offer was at once accepted by Cyrus McCormick, and as the second field was fairly level, he laid low six acres of wheat before sundown. This was no more than he had done in 1831, but on this occasion he had conquered a larger and more incredulous audience.

After the sixth acre was cut, the Reaper was driven with great acclaim into the town of Lexington and placed on view in the court-house square. Here it was carefully studied by a

Professor Bradshaw of the Lexington Female Academy, who finally announced in a loud and emphatic voice, "This — machine — is worth — a hundred — thousand — dollars." This praise, from "a scholar and a gentleman," as McCormick afterwards called him, ·· as very encouraging. And still more so was the quiet word of praise from Robert McCormick, who said, "It makes me feel proud to have a son do what I could not do."

Of all who were present on that memorable summer day, not one is now alive. Neither in Lexington nor in Staunton — the towns that lay on either side of the McCormick farm — can we find any one who saw the Reapers of 1831 and 1832. But among those who testified at various lawsuits that they had seen the Lexington Reaper operate were Colonel James McDowell, Colonel John Bowyer, Colonel Samuel Reed, Colonel A. T. Barclay, Dr. Taylor, William Taylor. John Ruff, John W. Houghawout, John Steele, James Moore, and Andrew Wallace. There was an old lady, also, in 1885, Miss Polly Carson, who told how she had seen the Reaper hauled along the road by two horses, which, she said, "had to be led by a couple of darkies, because they were scared to death by the racket of the machine." And she expressed the general unbelief of that day, very likely, by saying, "I thought it was a right smart curious sort of a thing, but that it would n't come to much."

Cyrus McCormick was far from being the first to secure a Reaper patent. He was the forty-seventh. Twenty-three others in Europe and twenty-three in the United States had invented machines of varying inefficiency; but there was not one of these which could have been improved into the proper shape. Without any exception, the rival manufacturers who rose up in later years to fight McCormick did him the homage of copying his Reaper; and certainly none of them attempted to offer for sale any type of machine that was invented prior to 1831.

A careful study of the pre-McCormick Reapers reveals one fault common to all,— they were made by theorists, to cut ideal grain in ideal fields. Some of them, if grain always grew straight and was perfectly willing to be cut, might have been fairly useful. They assuredly might have succeeded if grain grew in a parlor. But to cut actual grain in actual fields was another matter, and quite beyond their power. None of them, apparently, knew the fundamental difference between a Reaper and a mower. They did not observe that grain is easy to cut but hard to handle, while grass is hard to cut and easy to handle; and they persisted in the assumption that grain could be reaped by a mower.

These inventors who failed, but who doubtless blazed the way by their failures to the final success of McCormick, were not, as he was, a practical farmer on rough and hilly ground. One was a clergyman, who devised a six-wheel chariot, with many pairs of scissors, and which was to be pushed by horses and steered by a rudder that in rough ground would jerk a man's arm out of joint. A second of these inventors was a sailor, who experimented with a few stalks of straight grain stuck in gimlet holes in his workshop floor. A third was an actor,

INTERIOR OF BLACKSMITH SHOP IN WHICH C. H. McCORMICK BUILT HIS
FIRST REAPER

who had built a Reaper that would cut artificial grain on the stage. A fourth was a school-teacher, a fifth a machinist, and so on. In no instance can we find that any one of these pre-McCormick inventors was a farmer, who therefore knew what practical difficulties had to be overcome.

The farmers, on the other hand, thought first of these difficulties and scoffed at the parlor inventors. The editor of the "Farmer's Register" spoke the opinion of most farmers of that time when he said that "an insurmountable difficulty will sometimes be found to the use of reaping-machines in the state of the growing crops, which may be twisted and laid flat in every possible direction. A whole crop may be ravelled and beaten down by high winds and heavy rains in a single day."

One of the basic reasons, therefore, for the success of Cyrus McCormick was the fact that he was not a parlor inventor. He was primarily a farmer. He knew what wheat was and how it grew. And his first aim in making a reaper was not to produce a mechanical curiosity, nor to derive a fortune from the sale of his patent, but to cut the grain on his father's farm.

So far as the pre-McCormick inventors are concerned, the whole truth about them seems to be that a few invented fractional mowers or reapers that were fairly good as far as they went, and that most of them invented nothing that became of any lasting value. Nine-tenths of them were pathfinders in the sense that they showed what ought *not* to be done.

Very little attention would have been given them had it not been for the persistent effort made by rival manufacturers to detract from McCormick's reputation as an inventor. This they did in a wholly impersonal manner, of course, so that they should not be obliged to pay him royalties, and because his prestige as the original inventor of the Reaper enabled him to outsell them among the farmers.

But now that the competition of Reaper manufacturers has been tempered by consolidation, the time has arrived to do justice to Cyrus McCormick as the inventor of the Reaper. The stock phrase,— "He was less of an inventor than a business man," which was so widely used against him during his lifetime, ought now in all fairness to be laid aside. The fact is, as we have seen, that he was schooled as a boy into an inventive habit of mind; and that before his invention of the Reaper, he had devised a new grain-cradle, a hillside plow, and a self-sharpening plow. There is abundant corroborative evidence in the letters which he wrote to his father and brothers, instructing them to "make the divider and wheel post longer," to "put the crank one inch farther back," and so forth. Also, in the will of Robert McCormick, there is a clause authorizing the executor to pay a royalty to Cyrus of fifteen dollars apiece on whatever machines were sold by the family during that season, showing that the father, who of all men was in the best position to know, regarded Cyrus as the inventor.

Of all the manufacturers who fought Mc-Cormick in the patent suits of early days, three only have survived to see the passing of the Mc-Cormick Centenary — Ralph Emerson, C. W. Marsh, and William N. Whiteley. In response to a question as to Cyrus McCormick's place as an inventor, Mr. Whiteley said: "McCormick invented the divider and the practical reel; and he was the first man to make the Reaper a success in the field." Mr. Marsh said: "He was a meritorious inventor, although he combined the ideas of other men with his own; and he produced the first practical side-delivery machine in the market." And Mr. Emerson said: "The enemies of Cyrus H. McCormick have said that he was not an inventor, but I say that he was an inventor of eminence."

Thus it appears that the invention of the Reaper was not in any sense unique; it came about by an evolutionary process such as produced all other great discoveries and inventions. First come the dreamers, the theorists, the heroic innovators who awaken the world's brain upon a new line of thought. Then come the pioneers who solve certain parts of the problem and make suggestions that are of practical value. And then, in the fulness of time, comes one masterful man who is more of a doer than a dreamer, who works out the exact combination of ideas to produce the result, and establishes the new product as a necessary part of the equipment of the whole human family.

Cyrus Hall McCormick invented the Reaper. He did more — he invented the business of making Reapers and selling them to the farmers of America and foreign countries. He held preëminence in this line, with scarcely a break, until his death; and the manufacturing plant that he founded is to-day the largest of its kind. Thus, it is no more than an exact statement of the truth to say that he did more than any other member of the human race to abolish the famine of the cities and the drudgery of the farm — to feed the hungry and straighten the bent backs of the world.

CHAPTER IV

IN 1831 Cyrus McCormick had his Reaper, but the great world knew nothing of it. None of the 850 papers that were being printed at this time in the United States had given the notice of its birth. There was the young inventor, with the one machine that the human race most needed, in a remote cleft of the Virginian mountains, four days' journey from Richmond, and wholly without any experience or money or influence that would enable him to announce what he had done.

He had such a problem to solve as no inventor of to-day or to-morrow can have. He was not living, as we are, in an age of faith and optimism — when every new invention is welcomed with a shout of joy. He confronted a sceptical and slow-moving little world, so different from that of to-day that it requires a few lines of portrayal.

In general, it was a non-inventive and hand-labor world. There were few factories, except for the weaving of cotton and woollen cloth. There was no sewing-machine, nor Bessemer converter, nor Hoe press, nor telegraph, nor photography. It was still the age of the tallow candle and stage-coach and tinder-box. Practically no such thing was known as farm machinery. Jethro Wood had invented his iron plow, but he was at this time dying in poverty, never having been able to persuade farmers to abandon their plows of wood. As for steel plows, no one in any country had conceived of such a thing. James Oliver was a bare-footed school-boy in Scotland and John Deere was a young blacksmith in Vermont. Plows were pulled by oxen and horses, not by slaves, as in certain regions of Asia; but almost every other sort of farm work was done by hand.

Railways were few and of little account. Eighty-two miles of flimsy track had been built in the United States; the Baltimore and Ohio was making a solemn experiment with loco-motives, horses, and *sails*, to ascertain which one of these three was the best method of propulsion. The first really successful American loco-

motive was put on the rails in this year; and
Professor Joseph Henry set up his trial telegraph
wire and gave the electric current its first lesson
in obedience.

There was no free library in the world in 1831.
The first one was started in Peterborough, N. H.,
two years later. In England, electoral reform
had not begun, a General Fast had been ordered
because of the prevalence of cholera, and a four-
pound loaf cost more than the day's pay of a
laborer. The United States was a twenty-four-
State republic, with very little knowledge of
two-thirds of its own territory. The source of
the Mississippi River, for instance, was unknown. To send a letter from Boston to New
York cost the price of half a bushel of wheat.
There was no newspaper in Wisconsin and no
house in Iowa. The first sale of lots was announced in Chicago, but there was then no public
building in that hamlet, nothing but a few log
cabins in a swampy waste that was populous
only in wild ducks, bears, and wolves. Forty
of the latter were shot by the villagers in 1834.

Of the many eminent men who had the same

REAPING WITH CRUDE KNIVES IN INDIA

birth-year as McCormick, Poe and Mendelssohn had begun to be known as men of genius in 1831. But Lincoln was then "a sort of clerk" in a village store. Darwin was setting out on H. M. S. *Beagle* upon his first voyage as a naturalist. Gladstone was a student at Oxford. Proudhon was working at the case as a poor printer. Oliver Wendell Holmes was somewhat aimlessly studying law. Chopin was on his way to Paris. Tennyson had left college, without a degree, to devote his life to the service of poetry. Three great men who had been born earlier, Garrison, Whittier, and Mazzini, began their life-work in 1831. And science was a babe in the cradle. Herbert Spencer, Virchow and Pasteur were learning the multiplication table. Huxley was six and Berthelot four.

There was no Kansas, Minnesota, Nebraska, California, nor Texas. Virginia was the main wheat State. Local famines were of yearly occurrence. The period between 1816 and 1820 had been one of severe depression and was bitterly referred to as the "1800-and-starve-to-death" period. Seventy-five thousand people had been imprisoned for debt in New York in a single year, and a workingmen's party had sprung up as a protest against such intolerable conditions. Even as late as 1837 there was a bread riot in the city of New York. Five thousand hungry rioters broke into the warehouse of Eli Hart & Company, and destroyed a great quantity of flour and wheat. Five hundred barrels of flour were thrown from the windows; and women and children gathered it up greedily from the dirty gutter where it fell.

So the world that confronted Cyrus McCormick was not a friendly world of science and invention and prosperity. It was slow and dull and largely hostile to whoever would teach it a better way of working. And we shall now see by what means McCormick compelled it to accept his Reaper, and to give him the credit and pay for his invention.

He was resolved from the first not to be robbed and flung aside as most inventors had been. Whitney, the inventor of the cotton-gin, had said in 1812: "The whole amount I have received is not equal to the value of the labor saved

in one hour by my machines now in use." Fulton
had died at fifty, plagued and plundered by
imitators. Kay, Jacquard, Heathcoat, and Har-
greaves, inventors of weaving machinery, were
mobbed. Arkwright's mill was burned by in-
cendiaries. Gutenberg, Cort, and Jethro Wood
lost their fortunes. Palissy was thrown into the
Bastile. And Goodyear, who gave us rubber,
Bottgher, who gave us Sèvres porcelain, and
Sauvage, who gave us the screw propeller, died
in poverty and neglect.

But Cyrus McCormick was more than an
inventor. He was a business-builder. In the
same resolute, deliberate way in which he had
made his Reaper, he now set to work to make a
business. He planned and figured and made
experiments. "His whole soul was wrapped up
in his Reaper," said one of the neighbors. Once
while riding home on horseback in the Summer
of 1832, his horse stopped to drink in the centre
of a stream, and as he looked out upon the fields
of yellow grain, shimmering in the sunlight, the
dazzling thought flashed upon his brain, "Perhaps I may make a million dollars from this

Reaper." As he said in a letter written in later
years: "This thought was so enormous that it
seemed like a dream-like dwelling in the clouds
— so remote, so unattainable, so exalted, so
visionary."

His first step was seemingly a mistake, though
it must have contributed much toward the
development of self-reliance and hardihood in
his own character. He received a tract of land
from his father, and proceeded with might and
main to farm it alone. There was a small log
house on his land, and here he lived with two
aged negro servants and his Reaper.

He needed money to buy iron — to advertise
— to appoint agents. And he had no means
of earning money except by farming.

It is very evident that he had not set aside
his purpose to make Reapers, for we find in
the *Lexington Union* of September 28, 1833,
the first advertisement of his machine. He
offers Reapers for sale at $50.00 apiece, and
gives four testimonials from farmers. But nothing came of this advertisement. No farmer came

forward to buy. The four men who had given testimonials had only seen the Reaper at work. They were not purchasers. McCormick was "a voice crying in the wilderness" for *nine years* before he found a farmer who had the money and the courage to buy one of his Reapers.

After living for more than a year on his farm, McCormick saw that as a means of raising money it was a failure. It had given him a most valuable period of preparatory solitude, but it had not helped him to launch the Reaper; so he looked about him for some enterprise that would yield a larger profit. There was a large deposit of iron ore near by, and he resolved to build a furnace and make iron. Iron was the most expensive item in the making of a reaper. At that time it was $50.00 a ton — two and a half cents a pound. So as he had been unable to establish the Reaper business with a farm, he now set out to do it with a furnace. He persuaded his father and the school teacher to become his partners; and they built the furnace and were making their first iron in 1835 — the same year, by the way, in which a babe named Andrew Carnegie was born in the little Scotch town of Dunfermline.

For several years the furnace did fairly well. It swallowed the ore and charcoal and limestone, and poured into the channelled sand little sputtering streams of fiery metal. Cyrus made the patterns for the moulds, and, because of his great strength, did much of the heaviest labor. But the work was so incessant that he had no time to build Reapers. And in 1839, when the effects of the 1837 panic were felt in the more remote regions of Virginia, Cyrus McCormick realized to the full the aptness of that couplet of Hudibras —

> "Ah, me, the perils that environ
> The man who meddles with cold iron!"

The price of iron fell; debtors were unable to pay; the school teacher signed over his property to his mother; and the whole burden of the inevitable bankruptcy fell upon the McCormicks. Cyrus gave up his farm to the creditors, and whatever other property he had that was saleable. He did not give up the Reaper, and

nobody would have taken it if he had. Thus far, he had made no progress towards the building of a Reaper business. Instead of being the owner of a million, or any part of a million, he was eight years older than when he had begun to seek his fortune, and penniless.

In this hour of debt and defeat Cyrus became the leader of the family. Here for the first time he showed that indomitable spirit which was, more than any other one thing, the secret of his success. At once he did what he had not felt was possible before — he began to make Reapers. Without money, without credit, without customers, he founded the first of the world's reaper factories in the little log workshop near his father's house. In the year of the iron failure, 1839, he gave a public exhibition on the farm of Joshua Smith, near the town of Staunton. With two men and a team of horses he cut two acres of wheat an hour. At this there was great applause, but no buyers.

The farmers of that day were not accustomed to the use of machinery. Their farm tools, for the most part, were so simple as to be made either by themselves or by the village black-smith. That the Reaper did the work of ten men, they could not deny. But it was driven by an expert. "It's all very wonderful, but I'm running a farm, not a circus," thought the average spectator at these exhibitions. Also, there was in all Eastern States at that time a surplus of labor and a scarcity of money, both of which tended to retard the adoption of the Reaper.

Neither did the business men of Staunton pay any serious attention to it. There was a Samson Eager at that time who made wagons, a David Gilkerson who made furniture, a Jacob Kurtz who made spinning wheels, and an Absalom Brooks who made harness. But none of these men saw any fortune in the making of Reapers, and Staunton lost its great opportunity to be a manufacturing centre.

Failure was being heaped on failure, yet Cyrus McCormick hung to his Reaper as John Knox had to his Bible. He went back to the little log workshop with a fighting hope in his heart, and hammered away to make a still better machine.

This was the darkest period in the history of the McCormicks — from 1837 to 1840. Once a constable named John Newton rode up to the farm-house door with a summons, calling Cyrus and his father before the County Judge on account of a debt of $19.01. A teamster named John Brains had brought suit. His bill had been $72.00 and he had been paid more than three-fourths of the money. But the constable was so impressed with the honesty and industry of the McCormicks, that he rode back to town without having served the summons. A little later, Mr. John Brains received his money; and it may be said that had he accepted, instead, a five per cent interest in the Reaper, he would have become in twenty years or less one of the richest men in the county.

As it happened, not one of Cyrus McCormick's creditors thought of such an idea as seizing the Reaper, or the patent, which had been secured in 1834. If the queer-looking

machine, which was regarded as part marvel
and part freak, had been put up to auction
in that neighborhood of farmers, very likely
it would have found no bidders. There
appeared to be one man only, a William
Massie, who appreciated the ability of Cyrus
McCormick and lent him sums of money on
various urgent occasions.

But in 1840 a stranger rode from the north
and drew rein in front of the little log workshop.
In appearance he was a rough-looking man, but
to Cyrus he was an angel of light. He had
come to buy a Reaper. He had been one of the
spectators at the Staunton exhibition, and he
had resolved to risk $50 on one of the new
machines. His name, which deserves to be
recorded in the annals of the Reaper, was
Abraham Smith.

Several weeks later came two other angels in
disguise — farmers who had heard of the Reaper
and who had ridden from their homes on the
James River, a forty-mile journey on horseback through the Blue Ridge Mountains. These
men had never seen a Reaper, but they had

REAPING WITH CRADLES IN ILLINOIS

faith.   They were notable men.   Both ordered
machines, and Cyrus McCormick accepted one
of the orders only, as he was not satisfied with
the way his Reaper worked in grain that was
wet.   It was apt to clog in the grooves that
held the blade.   Even in this darkest and most
debt-ridden period of his life, McCormick was
much more intent, apparently, upon making
his Reapers work well than upon winning a
fortune.

Almost breathlessly, the young inventor waited
for the next harvest.   This was the unique
difficulty of his task, that he had only a few
weeks once a year to try out his machine and to
improve it.   He had now sold two, so that
there were three Reapers clicking through the
grain-fields in the Summer of 1840.   They
failed to operate evenly.   Where the grain was
dry, they cut well; but where it was damp,
they clogged and at times refused to cut at all.

Wet grain!   This, after nine years of arduous
labor, still remained a stubborn obstacle to
the success of the Reaper.   It was especially
hard to overcome, because in that primitive

neighborhood McCormick could not secure the
best workmanship in the making of the cutting-
blade. However, this obstacle did not daunt
him. He gave his blade a more serrated edge,
and to his delight it cut down the wet grain
very nearly as neatly as the dry.

This success had cost him another year, for
he sold no machines in 1841. But he had now,
at least, a wholly satisfactory Reaper. Fortified
with a testimonial from Abraham Smith, he
fixed the price at $100 and became a salesman.
By great persistence he sold seven Reapers in
1842, twenty-nine in 1843, and fifty in 1844.
At last, after thirteen years of struggle and
defeat, Cyrus McCormick had succeeded; and
the home farm was transformed into a busy
and triumphant Reaper factory.

There were new obstacles, of course. A few
buyers failed to pay. Four machines were
held on loitering canal-boats until they were
too late for the harvest. There was strong
opposition in several places by day laborers.
A trusted workman who was sent out to collect
$300 ran away with both horse and money.

But none of these trifles moved the victorious McCormick. The great stubborn world was about to surrender, and he knew it.

By 1844 he had done more than sell machines. He had made converts. One enthusiastic farmer named James M. Hite, who had made a world's record in 1843 by cutting 175 acres of wheat in less than eight days, was the first of these apostles of the Reaper. "My Reaper has more than paid for itself in one harvest," he said; and he gave $1,333 for the right to sell Reapers in eight counties. Closely after this man came Colonel Tutwiler, who agreed to pay $2,500 for the right to sell in southern Virginia. And a manufacturer in Richmond, J. Parker, bought an agency in five counties for $500; and won the renown of being the first business man who appreciated the Reaper. All this money was not paid in at once. Some of it was never paid. But after thirteen years of struggle and debt, this was Big Business.

Best of all, orders for seven Reapers had come from the West. Two farmers in Tennessee and one each in Wisconsin, Missouri, Iowa,

Illinois, and Ohio, had written to McCormick
for "Virginia Reapers," as they were called in
the farm papers of that day. These seven
letters, as may be imagined, brought great joy
and satisfaction to the McCormick family,
which was now, under the leadership of Cyrus,
devoting its best energies to the making of
Reapers. The Reapers were made and then,
when the question of their transportation arose,
Cyrus for the first time saw clearly that the
Virginia farm was not the best site for a factory.
To get the seven Reapers to the West, they had
first to be carried in wagons to Scottsville, then
by canal to Richmond, re-shipped down the
James River to the Atlantic Ocean and around
Florida to New Orleans, transferred here to
a river boat that went up the Mississippi and
Ohio Rivers to Cincinnati, and from Cincinnati
in various directions to the expectant farmers.
Four of these Reapers arrived too late for the
harvest of 1844, and two of them were not paid
for. Clearly, something must be done to supply the Western farmers more efficiently

At this time a friend said to him, "Cyrus,

AN EARLY ADVERTISEMENT FOR McCORMICK'S PATENT VIRGINIA REAPER

why don't you go West with your Reaper,
where the land is level and labor is scarce?"
His mind was ripe for this idea. It was the call
of the West. So one morning he put $300 into
his belt and set off on a 3,000-mile journey
to establish the empire of the Reaper. Up
through Pennsylvania he rode by stage to Lake
Ontario, then westward through Ohio, Michigan, Illinois, Wisconsin, Iowa, and Missouri.

For the first time he saw the *prairies*. So
vast, so flat, so fertile, these boundless plains
amazed him. And he was quick to see that
this great land ocean was the natural home of
the Reaper. Virginia might, but the West
must, accept his new machine.

Already the West was in desperate need of a
quicker way to cut grain. As McCormick rode
through Illinois, he saw the most convincing
argument in favor of his Reaper. He saw hogs
and cattle turned into fields of ripe wheat, for
lack of laborers to gather it in. The fertile
soil had given Illinois five million bushels of
wheat, and it was too much. It was more than
the sickle and the scythe could cut. Men

toiled and sweltered to save the yellow affluence from destruction. They worked by day and by night; and their wives and children worked. But the tragic aspect of the grain crop is this — it must be gathered quickly or it breaks down and decays. It will not wait. The harvest season lasts from four to ten days only. And whoever cannot snatch his grain from the field during this short period must lose it.

Truly, the West needed the Reaper; and McCormick's first plan was to overcome the transportation obstacle by selling licenses to many manufacturers in many States. By 1846 he had, with herculean energy, started Fitch & Company and Seymour, Morgan & Company in Brockport, N. Y., Henry Bear in Missouri, Gray & Warner in Illinois, and A. C. Brown in Cincinnati. These manufacturers, and the McCormick family in Virginia, built 190 Reapers for the harvest of 1846. This was multiplying the business by four, very nearly, but the plan was not satisfactory. Some manufacturers used poor materials; some had unskilled workmen; and one became so absorbed in new experiments that when the harvest time arrived, his machines were not completed.

The new difficulty was not to get manufacturers to make Reapers, but to get them to make *good* Reapers. What was to be done? The thought of having defective Reapers scattered among the farmers was intolerable to Cyrus McCormick. He pondered deeply over the whole situation. He considered the fact that the supremacy in wheat was slowly passing from Virginia to Ohio. He took note of the railroads that were creeping westward. He remembered the limitless prairies, far out in the sunset country, that were still uncultivated. Plainly, he must make Reapers in a factory of his own, so as to have them made well, and he must locate that factory as near as possible to the prairies, at some point along the Great Lakes. With the most painstaking diligence he studied the map and finally he put his finger upon a town — a small new town, which bore the strange name of *Chicago*.

CHAPTER V

OF all the cities that Cyrus McCormick had seen in his 3,000-mile journey, Chicago was unquestionably the youngest, the ugliest, and the most forlorn. It lacked the comforts of ordinary life, and many of the necessities. For the most part, it was the residuum of a broken land boom; and most of its citizens were remaining in the hope that they might persuade some incoming stranger to buy them out.

The little community, which had absurdly been called a city ten years before, had at this time barely ten thousand people — as many as are now employed by a couple of its department stores. It was exhausted by a desperate struggle with mud, dust, floods, droughts, cholera, debt, panics, broken banks, and a slump in land values. Other cities ridiculed its ambitions and called it a mudhole. Its harbor, into which six small schooners ventured in 1847, was obstructed by a sand-bar. And the entire region, for miles back from the lake, was a dismal swamp — the natural home of frogs, wild ducks, and beavers.

The six years between 1837 and 1843 had been to Illinois a period of the deepest discouragement. There was little or no money that any one could accept with confidence. Trade was on a barter basis. The State was hopelessly in debt. It had borrowed $14,000,000 in the enthusiasm of its first land boom, and now had no money to pay the interest. Even as late as 1846 there was only $9,000 in the State treasury.

Buffalo was at this time the chief grain market of the United States. We were selling a little wheat to foreign countries — much less than is grown to-day in Oklahoma. Hulled corn was the staff of life in Iowa. The Mormons had just started from Illinois on their 1,500-mile pilgrimage to the West, through a country that had not a road, a village, a bridge, nor a well. The sewing-machine had recently been invented by Howe, and the use of ether had been announced by Dr. Morton; but there was no Hoe press, nor Bessemer steel, nor even so much as a postage stamp. And in the Old World the two most impressive figures, perhaps, were Livingstone, the missionary, who was groping his way to the heart of the Dark Continent, and De-Lesseps, the master-builder of canals, who was now cutting a channel through the hot sand at Suez.

In Chicago, there was at this time no Board of Trade. The first wheat had been exported nine years before — as much as would load an ordinary wagon. There was no paved street, except one short block of wooden paving. The houses were rickety, unpainted frame shanties, which had not even the dignity of being numbered. There was a school, a jail, a police force of six, a theatre, and a fire-engine. But there was no railroad, nor telegraph, nor gas, nor sewer, nor stock-yards. The only post-office was a little frame shack on Clark Street, with one window and one clerk; and one of the lesser hardships of the citizens was to stand in line here on rainy days.

Prosperity was still an elusive hope in 1847, but the spirit of depression was being overcome.

THE McCORMICK REAPER OF 1847, ON WHICH SEATS WERE PLACED FOR THE DRIVER AND THE RAKER

The Federal bankrupt law of 1842 had broken the deadlock, and the Legislature had passed several "Hard Times" measures for the relief of debtors. To such an extent had the little community recovered its confidence that it opened a new theatre, welcomed its first circus, founded a law-school, launched a new daily paper called the *Tribune*, and organized a regiment for the Mexican War.

There were two Chicago events in this year which must have deeply impressed Cyrus Mc-Cormick. The first was the arrival of a horde of hunger-driven immigrants from Ireland. The famine of 1846, which had caused 210,000 deaths in that unfortunate island, was driving the survivors to America; and the people of Chicago showed the warmest sympathy towards these gaunt, sad-faced newcomers. Even in the depth of her own depression, Chicago called a special meeting to consider what could be done to alleviate the suffering of the Irish, and gave several thousand dollars for their relief.

The second event was the holding of the great "River and Harbor Convention" in Chicago.

This was the first formal recognition of Chicago by Congress, and gave the greatest possible amount of delight and reassurance to its citizens. Abraham Lincoln, who had just been elected to Congress, was there; and Horace Greeley and Thurlow Weed. There was a grand procession in the muddy little main street. A ship under full sail was hauled through the city on wheels. The newly organized firemen, in the glory of red shirts and leather hats, threw a stream of water over the flag-staff in the public square, and Thurlow Weed, in a peroration that aroused the utmost enthusiasm, prophesied that "on the shores of these lakes is a vast country that will in fifty years support one-quarter of a million people." It is interesting to notice that had Thurlow Weed lived fifty years after the delivery of that optimistic prophecy, he would have seen one-quarter of a million school children in the city of Chicago alone.

As a matter of history, the arrival of McCormick was a much more important event for Chicago than the "River and Harbor Convention." He was the first of its big manufacturers.

His factory was the largest and the busiest;
and the Reapers that it produced were a most
important factor in the growth of Chicago.
Every Reaper shipped to the West was a feeder
of the city. It brought back more wheat. It
opened up new territory. The Reaper gave the
farmers of the Middle West an ideal weapon
with which to win wealth from the prairies.
And it established the primary greatness
of Chicago as the principal wheat market of
the world.

This incoming flood of wheat gave Chicago
its start as a railway and shipping centre. Chicago was never obliged to give money, or to lend
it, to railroad companies. The railroads came
into Chicago without the inducement of sub-
sidies, because they wanted to carry its wheat.
And ships, too, came more and more readily to
Chicago when they found that they could be
sure of a return cargo.

The choice of Chicago as his centre of opera-
tions was one of the master-strokes of McCormick's career. At that time, Cleveland, Mil-
waukee, and St. Louis were more prosperous

cities; but McCormick considered one thing
only — the making and selling of his Reaper,
and he saw that Chicago, with all its mud and
shabbiness, was the link between the Great
Lakes and the Great West. Here he could best
assemble his materials — steel from Sheffield,
pig iron from Scotland and Pittsburg, and
white ash from Michigan. And here he could
best ship his finished machines to both East
and West.

Chicago, in fact, and the McCormick Reaper,
had many characteristics in common. Both
were born at very nearly the same time. Both
were cradled in adversity. Both were unsightly
to the artistic eye. Both were linked closely
with the development of the West. And both
inevitably achieved success, because they were
fundamentally right — Chicago in location and
the Reaper in design.

At the time that he began to build his Chicago
factory, Cyrus McCormick was no longer a
country youth. He was thirty-eight years of
age, and a tall powerful Titan of a man, with
a massive head and broad shoulders. His

upper lip was clean-shaven, but he had a thick, well-trimmed beard, and dark, wavy hair, worn fairly long. His nose was straight and well-shaped, his mouth firm, and his eyes brown-gray and piercing. In manner he was resolute and prompt, with a rigid insistence that could not be turned aside. He had won the prize in the contest of reaper-inventors; and he was now about to enter a second contest, against overwhelming odds, with a number of aggressive and competent business men who had determined that, by right or by might, they would manufacture McCormick Reapers and sell them to the farmers.

As McCormick had neither money nor credit, it was evident to him that his first step in busi-ness-building must be to secure a partner who had both of these. He looked about him and selected the man who was unquestionably the first citizen of Chicago — William B. Ogden. Ogden had been the first mayor of the little city. He had been from the beginning its natural leader. He had built the first handsome house, promoted the first canal, and was now busy in

the building of the first railroad from Chicago
to Galena.

William Butler Ogden had been born in the
little New York hamlet of Walton, four years
earlier than the birth of McCormick. To use
his own picturesque words, he "was born close
to a saw-mill, was early left an orphan, chris-
tened in a mill-pond, taught at a log school-
house, and at fourteen fancied that nothing was
impossible, which ever since, and with some
success, I have been trying to prove." Once
in Chicago he quickly made a fortune in
real estate, and was generally looked to as the
leader in any large enterprise that promised
to help Chicago.

He was a tall man of striking appearance.
At that time he wore no beard, and with his
keen eyes, high forehead, long straight nose,
and masterful under-lip, he would attract
attention in any assemblage. By his hospi-
tality and courtly manners he made many
friends for the city. Among his guests were
Webster, Van Buren, Bryant, Tilden, and Miss
Martineau. And when Cyrus McCormick

CYRUS HALL McCORMICK

From a Daguerreotype, taken about 1839

came to him and proposed the building of a
Reaper factory, Ogden was as quick as a flash
to see its value to Chicago. "You are the man
we want," said he to McCormick. "I 'll give
you $25,000 for a half interest, and we 'll start
to build the factory at once."

This partnership helped McCormick greatly.
It gave him at once capital, credit, prestige,
and a factory. It enabled him to escape from
the tyranny of small anxieties. It set him free
from contract-breaking manufacturers, who
looked upon the making of Reapers merely as
business, and not, as McCormick did, as a mis-
sion. He now had his chance to manufacture
on a large scale; and he immediately made
plans to sell 500 Reapers for the harvest of 1848.
He built the largest factory in Chicago, on the
spot where John Kinzie had built the first
house in 1804, and thus once for all was solved
the problem of where and how his Reapers
should be made.

For two years it was one of the sights of
Chicago to see McCormick and Ogden walking
together to their factory. They were both tall,

powerful, dominating men, and were easily the chief citizens — the Romulus and Remus of a city that was destined to be more populous than Rome.

But they were not suited as co-workers. Each was too strong-willed for co-operative action. Also, Ogden was a man of many interests, while McCormick was absorbed in his Reaper. There was no open quarrel, but in 1849 McCormick said: "I will pay you back the $25,000 that you invested, and give you $25,000 for profits and interest." Ogden accepted, well pleased to have doubled his money in two years; and from that time onward McCormick had no partners except the members of his own family.

Moving at once from one obstacle to another, as McCormick did throughout the whole course of his life, he now began to create the best possible *system* of selling his Reapers to the farmers. This he had to do, for the reason that there was no means at that time whereby he could offer them for sale. The village blacksmith was too busy at his anvil to become an

agent. The village storekeeper was not a
mechanic, and was too careful of his reputation
among the farmers to offer for sale a machine
that he did not understand. Therefore, Mc-
Cormick bent all his energies to this new task
of devising a mode of action. He began to
develop what he was apt to call "the finger-ends
of the business." And he created a new species
of commercial organization which is by many
thought to be fully as remarkable as his invention of the Reaper.

First, he gave a *Written Guarantee* with every
machine. He had conceived of this inducement
as early as 1842. He "warranted the per-
formance of the Reaper in every respect," and
by this means made seven sales in that year.
In 1848 he had his guarantee printed like an
advertisement, with a picture of the Reaper at
the top, and blank spaces for the farmer, the
agent, and two witnesses to sign. The price
of the machine was to be $120. The farmer
was to pay $30 cash, and the balance in six
months, on condition that the Reaper would
cut one and a half acres an hour, that it would

scatter less grain than the grain-cradle, that
it was well made, and that the raking off
could easily be done from a raker's seat.
If the Reaper failed to fulfil these promises,
it was to be brought back and the $30 was
to be refunded.

This idea of giving a free trial, and returning
the money to any dissatisfied customer, was at
that time new and revolutionary. To-day it is
the code of the department store, and even the
mail-order establishments are in many instances
adopting it. It has become one of the higher
laws of the business world. It has driven that
discreditable maxim, "Let the buyer beware,"
out of all decent commercialism. To Mc-
Cormick, who had never studied the selfish
economic theories of his day, there was no
reason for any antagonism between buyer and
seller. He trusted his Reaper and he trusted
the farmers. And he built his business four-
square on this confidence.

Second, he sold his Reapers at a *Known
Price.* He announced the price in newspapers
and posters. This, too, has since become an

established rule in business; but it was not so sixty years ago. The Oriental method of chaffering and bargaining was largely in vogue. The buyer got as high a price as he could in each case. Among merchants, A. T. Stewart was probably the first to abolish this practice of haggling, and to mark his goods in plain figures. And in the selling of farm machinery, it was McCormick who laid down the principle of equal prices to all and special rebates to none — a principle which has been very generally followed ever since, except during periods of over-strenuous competition.

Third, he was one of the first American business men who believed heartily in a policy of *Publicity.* As early as September 28, 1833, he began to advertise his Reaper; and his advertisement was nearly a column in length. Also, in the same paper, he had a half-column advertisement of his hillside plow. This was publicity on a large scale, according to the ideas of advertising that were then prevalent. Even George Washington, when advertising an extensive land scheme in 1773, had not thought

of using more than half a column of a Baltimore paper.

McCormick was an efficient advertiser, too,
as well as an enterprising one. When he talked
to farmers, he knew what to say. He told
the story of what one of his Reapers had done,
and named the time and the farm and the
farmers. He made great use of the argument
that the Reaper pays for itself, and showed that
it would cost the farmer less to buy it than *not*
to buy it.

Among the many testimonials that he got
from farmers the one that pleased him most,
and which he scattered broadcast, was one in
which a farmer said: "My Reaper has more
than paid for itself in one harvest."

In 1849, when the rush to the new gold mines
of California began, he was quick to see his
opportunity. This sudden exodus of a hundred
thousand men to the Pacific coast meant much
to him, and he knew it. It meant a decrease
in the number of farm laborers and an increase in the amount of money in circulation.

PANORAMIC VIEW SHOWING THE McCORMICK REAPER WORKS BEFORE THE

CHICAGO FIRE OF 1871, ON CHICAGO RIVER, EAST OF RUSH STREET BRIDGE

More than this, it meant that Chicago was no longer a city of the Far West. It was *central*. It was the link between the banks and factories of the East and the gold mines and prairies of the West. So McCormick quickly prepared an elaborate advertisement, warning the farmers that labor would now become scarce and expensive, that the coming grain crop promised to be a large one, and giving the names and addresses of ninety-two farmers who were now using his machines.

The fourth factor in the McCormick System was the appointment of a *Responsible Agent* and the building of a storage warehouse at every competitive point. He did not wait for the business to grow. He pushed it. He thrust it forward by sending an agent to every danger-spot on the firing-line. As one of his competitors complained, in an 1848 lawsuit, McCormick "flooded the country with his machines." He knew that many farmers would be undecided until the very hour of harvest, when there would be no time to get a Reaper from Chicago;

and therefore he had supplies of machines stored in various parts of the country. By 1849 he had nineteen of these agencies.

His plan, with regard to these agents, was to fasten them to him by exclusive contracts, which forbade them to sell Reapers made by any other manufacturers. Each agent was given free scope. He was not worried by detail instructions. He was picked out for his aggressive, self-reliant qualities, and the whole responsibility of a certain territory was put upon him. Once a month he made a report; but he stood or fell by the final showing for the year, which he made in October. This plan of leaving his men free and putting them upon their mettle, developed their mental muscle to the utmost. Also, it made them intensely loyal and combative — a regiment, not of private soldiers, but generals, each one in charge of his own province, blamed for his defeats and rewarded for his victories.

The fifth factor in the McCormick System was the *Customers' Good-Will.* For the good-will of other capitalists or for the applause of

the public in general, no men cared less than
McCormick. But he always stood well with
the farmers. "I have never yet sued a farmer
for the price of a Reaper," he said in 1848. This
heroic policy he pursued as long as possible,
knowing the fear that all farmers have of contracts that may lead them into litigation. More
than this, he freely gave them credit, without
being safeguarded by any Dun or Bradstreet.
He allowed them to pay with the money that
was saved during the harvest. "It is better
that I should wait for the money," he said,
"than that you should wait for the machine
that you need." So he borrowed money in
Chicago to build the Reapers, borrowed more
money to pay the freight, and then sold them
on time to the farmers.

In some cases he lost heavily, as in Kansas
and North Dakota, where the first settlers were
driven off by drought. But as a rule he lost little
by bad debts. Immigrants of twenty nationali-
ties swarmed westward upon the free land offered
to them by the United States Government, and
usually each man found waiting for him at the

nearest town one of the McCormick agents, ready to supply him with a Reaper, whether he had the money to pay for it or not. As may be imagined, the effect of this policy upon the settlement and welfare of the West was magical. There are to-day tens of thousands of Western farmers who date the era of their prosperity from the day when a McCormick Reaper arrived in all the glory of its red paint and shining blade, and held its first reception in the barn-yard.

One instance of this deserves to be embodied in the history of the Reaper. In 1855 a poor tenant farmer, who had been evicted from his rented land in Ayrshire, Scotland, arrived with his family at the banks of the Mississippi. There was then no railroad nor stage-coach, so the whole family walked to a quarter section of land farther west, not far from where the city of Des Moines stands to-day. The first year they cut the wheat with the cradle and the scythe, and the following year they bought a McCormick Reaper. They prospered. The father went back for a visit to Ayrshire and paid all his creditors. And the eldest son, James, became first Speaker of the Iowa Legislature, then a professor in an agricultural college, and finally the founder of the Department of Agriculture in all its present completeness. To-day we know him as the Honorable James Wilson, the first official farmer of the United States.

There was one other method in the marketing of farm machinery, which seems to have been originated by McCormick — the *Field Test*. As a means of stirring up interest in an indifferent community, this was the most electrical in its effects of any plan that has ever been devised. As a pioneering advertisement, it was unsurpassed. It was nothing less than a contest in a field of ripe grain between several machines that belonged to rival manufacturers. Sometimes there were only two machines, and in one grand tournament there were forty. And all the farmers in the county were invited to come and witness the battle free of charge.

The first of these field tests occurred near Richmond in 1844. McCormick had challenged Obed Hussey, a Baltimore sailor who had invented a practical mowing-machine, and who was offering it for sale to cut grain as well as grass. In this instance McCormick won easily. The judges said that while the Hussey machine was stronger and simpler, having no reel nor divider, the McCormick Reaper was lighter, cheaper, scattered less grain, and was better at cutting grain that was wet and in its method of delivering the grain.

"Meet Hussey whenever you can and put him down," Cyrus McCormick wrote to his brothers. In one letter, written the following year, he is so enthusiastically aggressive in the pursuit of Hussey that he proposes to his brothers a grand final contest. Hussey is to be dared to sign an agreement that in case of defeat, he will pay McCormick $10,000 and become the Maryland agent for the McCormick Reaper. McCormick, on his part, is to agree that if he is beaten he will pay Hussey $10,000 and become the Virginia agent for the Hussey machine. Nothing came of this confident proposal, either because it was not put into effect by McCormick, or because Hussey refused to accept it.

But the field test flourished for more than

forty years. It did more in the earlier days
than any other one thing to make talk about
the Reaper and to move the farmers out of the
old-fashioned ruts. It provided the vaudeville
element which is necessary in salesmanship
where people are not interested in the commod-
ity itself. As often happens, it was in the end
carried too far. It became the most costly
weapon of competition. It introduced all manner of unfairness and often violence. The most
absurd tests were frequently agreed to. Mowers
would be chained back to back and then forcibly
torn apart. Reapers were driven into groves
of saplings. Machines of special strength were
made secretly. And so the warfare raged, until
by general consent the field test was abandoned.

These six factors of the McCormick System
became the six commandments of the farm
machinery business. They were largely adopted
by his competitors, and exist to-day, with the
exception of the exclusive contract and the field
test.

By 1850 McCormick had not only solved
the problem of the Reaper; he had worked out

a method of distribution.   He had established
a new business.   But even this was not enough.
He was now beset by a swarm of manufacturers
who sought to deprive him of his patents and
of a business which he naturally regarded as his
own.   It remained to be seen whether he could
stand his ground when opposed by several hundred rivals; and whether he could duplicate in
the courts the victories that he had won in the
fields.

CHAPTER VI

THE STRUGGLE TO PROTECT PATENTS

IN 1848 Cyrus McCormick's original patent expired. He applied to have it extended, and at once there began one of the most extraordinary legal wars ever known in the history of the Patent Office. It continued with very little cessation until 1865. It enlisted on one side or the other the ablest lawyers of that period — such giants of the bar as Lincoln, Stanton, Seward, Douglas, Harding, Watson, Dickerson, and Beverdy Johnson. The tide of battle rolled from court to court until the final clash came in the chamber of the Supreme Court and the halls of Congress. It was perhaps the most Titanic effort that any American inventor has ever made to protect his rights and to carry out the purpose of the Patent Law.

McCormick had strong reasons for believing that his patent should be extended. He was asking for no more than the Patent Office, on other occasions, had granted to other inventors.

A patent was supposed to protect an inventor for fourteen years, and he had lost half of this time in making a better machine, and in finding out the best way to carry on the business. He had received from all sources nearly $24,000, and most of it had been swallowed up in expenses. He was still a poor man in 1848. He was no more than on the threshold of prosperity. And his peculiar difficulty, which gave him a special claim upon the Patent Commissioners, was the shortness of the harvest season. He had only three or four weeks in each year in which he could make experiments.

For eight years McCormick's claim was tossed back and forth like a tennis ball between the Patent Office and Congress. This delay threw the door wide open to competition. A score of manufacturers built factories and began to make McCormick Reapers, with trifling variations and under other names. If McCormick had won his case, they would have had to pay him a royalty of $25 on each machine. Consequently, they combined against him. They hired lawyers and lobbyists, secured petitions from farmers, and raised a hue and cry that one man was "trying to impose a tax of $500,000 a year upon the starving millions of the world."

One firm of lawyers in Cincinnati sent a letter to these manufacturers in 1850, saying that, "McCormick can be beaten in the Patent Office, and must be beaten now or never. If funds are furnished us, we shall surely beat him; but if they are not furnished us, he will as certainly beat us. Please, therefore, take hold and help us to beat the *common enemy*. The subscriptions have ranged from $100 to $1,000. . Send in also to Patent Office hundreds of remonstrances like this: We oppose the extension of C. H. McCormick's patent. He has made money enough off of the farmer."

Towards the end of this famous case, the anti-McCormick lobby at the Capitol became so rabid that Senator Brown, of Mississippi, made an indignant protest on the floor of the Senate. He said: "Why, Mr. President, if it were not for the people out of doors, people without inventive genius, people without the genius to invent a mouse-trap or a fly-killer, who are pirating on the great invention of McCormick, there would never have been an hour's delay in granting all that he asks. I know, and I state here, in the face of the American Senate and the world, that these men have beset me at every corner of the street with their papers and their affidavits — men who have no claim to the ear of the country, men who have rendered it no service, but who have invested their paltry dollars in the production of a machine which sprang from the mind of another man; and who now, for their own gain, employ lawyers to draw cunning affidavits, to devise cunning schemes, and to put on foot all sorts of machinery to defeat McCormick."

What worried McCormick most was not this consolidation of competitors, but the fact that a few farmers had signed petitions of protest against his claim. This was "the most unkindest cut of all." But he made no attack upon them. Manufacturers he would fight, and inventors and lawyers and judges — any one and every one, if need be, except farmers. "How can the farmers be against me?" he asked in amazement. "They save the price of the Reaper in a single harvest."

McCormick lost his suit, as he did a second time in 1859, and a third time in 1861. Not one of his patents was at any time renewed. Up to 1858 he had received $40,000 in royalties, but it had cost him $90,000 in litigation. From first to last he did not get one dollar of net profit from the protection of the Patent Office.

Many other inventors were fairly treated by Congress. Fulton, for example, was presented with a bonus of $76,300. Willmoth, who improved the turret of a battleship, received $50,-000. Professor Page, for making an electric engine, was given $20,000. Morse was awarded $38,000. The patents of Goodyear, Kelly, Howe, Morse, Hyatt, Woodworth, and Blanchard were extended. The protection of inventors had been a national policy — an American tradition. In the phrasing of Daniel Webster: "The right of an inventor to his invention is a natural right, which existed before the Constitution was written and which is above the Constitution."

The benefit of the Reaper to the nation, and the fact that McCormick was its inventor, were admitted freely enough. Senator Johnson, of Maryland, estimated in 1858 that the Reaper was then worth to the United States $55,000,000 a year. D. P. Holloway, the Commissioner of Patents, sang an anthem of eloquent praise to McCormick in 1861. "He is an inventor whose fame, while he is yet living, has spread through the world," he said. "His genius has done honor to his own country, and has been the admiration of foreign nations. He will live in the grateful recollection of mankind as long as the reaping-machine is employed in gathering the harvest." Then, in an abrupt postscript to so fine a eulogy, this extraordinary Commissioner adds: "But the Reaper is of too great value to the public to be controlled by any individual, and the extension of his patent is refused."

The truth seems to be that McCormick was too strong, too aggressive, to receive fair play at the hands of any legislative body. The note of sympathy could never be struck in his favor. He personally directed his own cases.

PRINTING BY C. SCHUSSELE, PHILADELPHIA, 1=1

ENGRAVED ON STEEL, BY JOHN SARTAIN, PHILADELPHIA, 1862

MEN OF PROGRESS

STANDING, LEFT TO RIGHT: 1. Dr. W. T. G. Morton, first man to administer ether to a patient; 2. J. Bogardus, invented ring spinner (for cotton spinning), an engraving machine, and dry gas meter; 3. S. Colt, revolver; 4. Cyrus Hall McCormick, reaper; 5. Joseph Saxton, locomotive differential pulley and deep sea thermometer; 6. Peter Cooper, founder of Cooper Union and inventor machine for mortising hubs for carriage wheels; 7. Prof. J. Henry, inventor of communication by electricity; 8. E. B. Bigelow, power loom for spinning jenny.

SITTING, LEFT TO RIGHT: 1. C. Goodyear, vulcanizer of rubber; 2. J. L. Mott, iron manufacturer and inventor; 3. Dr. E. Nott, base burner for stoves; 4. F. E. Sickles, inventor of cut-off of steam in engine; 5. S. F. B. Morse, telegraph; 6. H. Burden, cultivator, and machine for making horseshoes; 7. R. M. Hoe, printing press; 8. I. Jennings; 9. T. Blanchard, machine for cutting and bending tacks, and lathe for turning irregular

He dominated his own lawyers. And he fought always in an old-fashioned, straight-from-the-shoulder way that put him at a great disadvantage in a legal conflict. Also, he was supposed to be much richer than in reality he was. He had made money by the rise in Chicago real estate. By 1866 he had become a millionaire. And his entire fortune was assumed by opposing lawyers to be the product of the Reaper business.

It is to be said, to the lasting honor of South Carolina, that she gave a grant of money to Whitney, out of the public treasury, as a token of gratitude for the invention of the cotton gin. But no wheat State ever gave, or proposed to give, any grant or vote of thanks to Cyrus McCormick for the invention of the Reaper. The business that he established was never at any time favored by a tariff, or franchise, or patent extension, or tax exemption, or land grant, or monopoly. Single-handed he built it up, and single-handed he held it against all comers. If, as Emerson has said, an institution is no more than "the lengthened shadow of one man," we

may fairly say that the immense McCormick
Company of to-day is no more than the lengthened shadow of this farm-bred Virginian.

By 1855 McCormick realized that the Federal
Government was not the impartial tribunal that
he had believed it to be. He saw that he could
not depend upon it for protection, so he made a
characteristic decision — he resolved to protect
himself. He, too, would hire a battery of lawyers and charge down upon these manufacturers
who were unrighteously making his Reaper and
depriving him of his patents. He engaged three
of the master lawyers of the American bar,
William H. Seward, E. N. Dickerson, and
Senator Reverdy Johnson, and brought suit
against Manny and Emerson, of Rockford,
Illinois, for making McCormick Reapers without a license.

Then came a three-year struggle that shook
the country and did much to shape the history
of the American people. Manny and Emerson,
who were shrewd and forceful men, hired twice
as many lawyers as McCormick and prepared
to defend themselves. They selected as the

members of this legal bodyguard, Abraham
Lincoln, Stephen A. Douglas, Edwin M. Stan-
ton, Peter H. Watson, George Harding, and
Congressman H. Winter Davis.

It was a battle of giants. Greek met Greek
with weapons of eloquence. But Stanton out-
classed his great co-debaters in a speech of
unanswerable power which unfortunately was
not reported. The speech so vividly impressed McCormick that in his next lawsuit he at once engaged Stanton. It awoke
the brain of Lincoln, as he afterwards admitted;
and drove him back to a more comprehensive
study of the law. It gave Lincoln so high
an opinion of Stanton's ability that, when he
became President several years later, he
chose Stanton to be his Secretary of War.
And it gripped judge and jury with such
effect that McCormick lost his case. It was
a wonderful speech.

Abraham Lincoln, who made no speech at
all, was the one who derived the most benefit in
the end from this lawsuit. It not only aroused
his ambitions, but gave him his first big fee —

$1,000. This money came to him at the precise moment when he needed it most, to enable him to enter into the famous debate with Douglas — the debate that made him the inevitable candidate of the Republican party. It is interesting to note how closely the destinies of Lincoln and McCormick were interwoven. Both were born in 1809, on farms in the South. Both struggled through a youth of adversity and first came into prominence in Illinois. Both labored to preserve the Union, and when the War of Secession came it was the Reaper that enabled Lincoln to feed his armies. Both men were emancipators, the one from slavery and the other from famine; and both to-day sleep under the soil of Illinois. No other two Americans had heavier tasks than they, and none worked more mightily for the common good.

Of all McCormick's lawsuits, and they were many, the most extraordinary was the famous Baggage Case, which lasted for twenty-three years — from 1862 to 1885. It was probably the best single instance of the man's dogged tenacity in defence of a principle. The original cause

of this trial was a comedy of mishaps. A Mc-
Cormick family party of six, with nine trunks,
boarded a train at Philadelphia for Chicago.
The train was about to start, when the baggage-
master demanded pay for 200 pounds of surplus baggage. The amount was only $8.70,
but McCormick refused to pay it. He called his
family out of the train and ordered that his
trunks be taken off. The conductor refused to
hold the train, and the trunks were carried away.
Mr. McCormick at once saw the president of
the railroad, J. Edgar Thompson, who telegraphed an order for the trunks to be put off
at Pittsburg. The McCormicks set out for
Chicago by the next train. At Pittsburg they
learned that the trunks had been carried through
to Chicago. And the next day, in Chicago, when
McCormick went to the Fort Wayne depot, he
found it a mass of smoking cinders. It had
caught fire in the night, and the nine trunks had
been destroyed.

McCormick sued the railroad for $7,193 —
the value of the trunks and their contents. Repeatedly he won and repeatedly the railroad

appealed to higher courts. After twenty years the worn and battered case was carried up to the nine Justices of the United States Supreme Court. They decided for McCormick. But even then the railroad evaded payment for three years, until after McCormick's death. Then the president of the road signed a check for $18,060.79, which was the original value of the nine trunks plus twenty-three years' interest.

McCormick did not for a moment regard this case as trivial. It involved a principle. Once when a friend bantered him for fighting so hard over a small matter, he replied, "My conscience, sir! I don't know what would become of the American people if there were not some one to stand up for fair dealing." His victory did much to teach the railroads better manners and a finer consideration of the travelling public. Soon after the conclusion of the case, a trunk belonging to a relative of the McCormicks was destroyed on the New York Central. It value was $1,300, and one of the railroad's lawyers promptly sent a check, saying, "We don't want to have a lawsuit with the McCormicks."

For these numerous lawsuits McCormick paid a terrible price, both in money and friendship. He acquired a reputation as "a man who would law you to death." He brought down upon himself to a remarkable degree the hostility of his competitors, and prevented himself from receiving the full credit and prestige that he deserved. Instead of being revered as the father of the Reaper business, he was feared as an industrial Bismarck — a man of unyielding will and indomitable purpose, who regarded his competitors as a pack of trespassers in an empire that belonged by right to him.

The truth is that this situation did not arise because of the natural perversity of either McCormick or his competitors. In his later life, McCormick proved that he could co-operate with his equals in the most harmonious way, in a new business enterprise. His competitors, too, were for the most part men of ability and uprightness. Neither in their public nor private lives, was there any stain upon the honor of such men as Wood, Osborne, Adriance, Manny, Emerson, Huntley, Warder, Bushnell, Glessner,

Jones, and Lewis Miller. But these men were all newcomers. They were beardless striplings compared to McCormick. He had made and exhibited a successful Reaper twenty years before the first of them began. His father had grappled with the problem of the Reaper before most of them were born. It was inevitable, therefore, that there should have been an unspanable gap between the two points of view. McCormick stood alone because he *was* alone. He and the Reaper had grown up together in long hazardous years of pioneering, through ridicule and poverty and failure. It was his dream come true. And in the same spirit with which he had fought to create it, he also fought to hold it, and to protect it from men to whom it was not a dream and a life-mission, but a mere machine.

CHAPTER VII

THE EVOLUTION OF THE REAPER

O F all the varieties of difficulties that confronted Cyrus H. McCormick during his
strenuous life, the most baffling and disconcert-
ing difficulty was when his Reaper began to
grow. For fifteen years — from 1845 to 1860 —
it had remained unchanged except that seats
had been added for the raker and the driver.
It did no more than cut the grain and leave it
on the ground in loose bundles. It had abolished the sickler and the cradler; but there yet
remained the raker and the binder. Might it
not be possible, thought the restless American
brain, to abolish these also and leave no one but
the driver?

This at once became a most popular and
fascinating problem for inventors. There was
by this time everything to gain and nothing to
lose by improving the Reaper. There was no
opposition and no ridicule. To cut grain by
horse-power had become, of course, the only

proper way of cutting it. As many as 20,000 Reapers of all kinds were made in 1860; and McCormick's factory had grown to be the pride of Chicago. It was 90 by 150 feet in size, two stories high, and gave work to about a hundred and twenty men.

As early as 1852 a fantastic self-rake Reaper had been invented by a mechanical genius named Jearum Atkins. This man was a bedridden cripple, who, to while away the tiresome hours of his confinement, bought a McCormick Reaper, had it placed outside his window, and actually devised an attachment to it which automatically raked off the cut grain in bundles. It was a grotesque contrivance. The farmers nicknamed it the "Iron Man." It consisted of an upright post, with two revolving iron arms. These arms whirled stiffly around, windmill fashion, and scraped the grain from the platform to the ground.

An amusing anecdote of this machine was told by Henry Wallace, known to all farmers of the Middle West as the founder of *Wallace's Farmer*. "The first Reaper that my father bought," said Mr. Wallace, "was a McCormick machine that had an 'Iron Man' on it. The first day that it was driven into the grain it made such a clatter that the horses ran away. It was certainly a terrifying sight as it rattled through the wheat, with its long, rake-fingered arms flying and hurling the cut grain in the wildest disorder. It was as good as a chariot race in a circus to the crowd of farmers, who had come to see how the new machine would operate. The next day my father tried again. There had been rain during the night, and the heavy machine stuck fast in the mud. It had cost $300, but my father took the 'Iron Man' off, and during the remainder of that harvest we raked off the grain by hand."

A great variety of self-rake Reapers soon appeared, and after 1860 the farmers would buy no other kind. Thus a part of the problem had been solved. The raker was abolished. There now remained the much more difficult work of supplanting the binder — the man, or sometimes woman, who gathered up the bundles of cut grain, and, making a crude rope of the grain itself, bound it tightly around the middle, making what was called a sheaf. This was hard, back-breaking work, intolerable when the sun was hot, except to men of the strongest physique. It required not strength only, but skill. Ninety-nine farmers out of a hundred believed that it would always have to be done by hand. "How can it be possible," they asked, "that a machine which is being dragged by horses over a rough. field can at the same time be picking up grain and tying knots?"

Just then two young farmers near De Kalb came to the rescue by inventing a new species of machine. It was neither a Reaper nor a self-binder. It was half-way between the two. It was the missing link. It appeared that an inventor named Mann had taken a McCormick Reaper and built a moving platform upon it, in such a way that the grain was carried up to a wagon which was drawn alongside. These two young farmers had bought a Mann machine, and one of them, when he saw it in operation, originated a brilliant idea.

"Why should the grain be carried up to a

wagon?" he asked. "Why can't we put a
foot-board on the machine, for two of us to
stand on, and then bind the grain as fast as
it is carried up?"

This was the origin of the "Marsh Harvester,"
which held the field for ten years or longer. It
did not abolish the man who bound, but it gave
him a chance to work twice as fast. It compelled him to be quick. It saved him the trouble
of walking from bundle to bundle. It enabled
him to stand erect. And best of all, it put half
a dozen inventors on the right line of thought.
Plainly, what was needed now was to teach a
Marsh Harvester to tie knots.

One evening in 1874 a tall man, with a box
under his arm, walked diffidently up the steps
of the McCormick home in Chicago, and rang
the bell. He asked to see Mr. McCormick, and
was shown into the parlor, where he found Mr.
McCormick, sitting as usual in a large and
comfortable chair.

"My name is Withington," said the stranger.
"I live in Janesville, Wisconsin. I have here
a model of a machine that will automatically

bind grain." Now, it so happened that Mc Cormick had been kept awake nearly the whole of the previous night by a stubborn business problem. He could scarcely hold his eyelids apart. And when Withington was in the midst of his explanation, with the intentness of a born inventor, McCormick fell fast asleep.

At such a reception to his cherished machine, Withington lost heart. He was a gentle, sensitive man, easily rebuffed, and so, when McCormick aroused from his nap, Withington had departed and was on his way back to Wisconsin. For a few seconds McCormick was uncertain as to whether his visitor had been a reality or a dream. Then he awoke with a start into instant action. A great opportunity had come to him and he had let it slip. He was at this time making self-rake Reapers and Marsh Harvesters; but what he wanted — what every Reaper manufacturer wanted in 1874 — was a self-binder. He at once called to him one of his trusted workmen.

"I want you to go to Janesville," he said. "Find a man named Withington, and bring him to me by the first train that comes back to Chicago."

The next day Withington was brought back and treated with the utmost courtesy. McCormick studied his invention and found it to be a most remarkable mechanism. Two steel arms caught each bundle of grain, whirled a wire tightly around it, fastened the two ends together with a twist, cut it loose and tossed it to the ground. This self-binder was perfect in all its details — as neat and effective a machine as could be imagined. McCormick was delighted. At last, here was a machine that would abolish the binding of grain by hand.

A bargain was made with Withington on the spot; and the following July a self-binder was tried on the Sherwood farm, near Elgin, Illinois. It cut fifty acres of wheat and bound every bundle without a slip. From this time onwards no one was needed but a man, a boy, a girl, anybody, who could hold the reins and drive a team of horses. Of the ten or twelve sweating drudges who toiled in the harvest-field, all were now to be set free — the sicklers, cradlers, rakers, binders — every one except the driver, and he (or she) was to have the glory of riding on the triumphal chariot of a machine that did all the work itself.

"There were ten men working in my wheat-field in the old days," said an Illinois farmer. "But to-day our hired girl climbs upon the spring seat of a self-binder and does the whole business."

McCormick was not the first to make one of these magical machines. There was an able and enterprising manufacturer in New York State, Walter A. Wood, who in 1873 had made three Withington binders, under the super-vision of Sylvanus D. Locke, who had been a co-worker with Withington. McCormick had given Wood his start, as early as 1853, by selling him a license to make Reapers; and Wood, by his high personal qualities, had built up a most extensive business. But McCormick was the first to make self-binders upon a large scale. He made 50,000 of the Withington machines, and pushed them with irresistible energy.

He originated a new method of advertising

THE FIRST McCORMICK SELF-RAKE REAPING MACHINE

the self-binders among the farmers. Special flat-cars were provided for him by the railroads. Upon each one of these cars a binder was placed, in the charge of an expert. These cars, during the harvest season, were attached to ordinary freight trains: and whenever the train came to a busy wheat-field it was stopped for an hour or more, the self-binder was rushed from the car to the field, and an exhibition of its skill given to the wondering farmers. Then it was put back on its car, and the train resumed its leisurely course until it arrived at the next scene of harvesting.

The sensitive-natured inventor, Charles B. Withington, who gave such timely aid to McCormick, was one of the most romantic knights-errant of industry in his generation. Born near Akron a year before McCormick invented his Reaper, he was trained by his father to be a watchmaker. At fifteen, to earn some pocket-money, he went into the harvest field to bind grain. He was not robust, and the hard, stooping labor under a hot sun would sometimes bring the blood to his head in a hemorrhage.

There were times after the day's work was done when he was too weary to walk home, and would throw himself upon the stubble to rest.

At eighteen he set out to find his fortune in the far West, became a Forty-niner, drifted to Australia, and in 1855 came back to Janesville, Wisconsin, with three thousand dollars or more in his belt. All this money he proceeded to fritter away on the invention of a self-rake Reaper — "a crazy scheme," as the towns-people called it. As it happened, the whole southern region of Wisconsin was being stirred up at that time by the speeches of an inventive Madison editor, who went by the name of "Pump" Carpenter. Carpenter's hobby was that the binding of grain must be done by machinery. He was eloquent and popular, and his arguments were substantiated by a little model which he was accustomed to carry about with him. Withington heard him speak and was converted. He dropped his self-rake reaper and went to work upon a self-binder. He completed his first machine in 1872, and was thrust from one discouragement to another until two years later he met McCormick.

It is a most interesting fact, and certainly not an accidental one, that the group of noted inventors who together produced the self-binder all appeared from the region south of Madison, which had been so aroused by the eloquence of "Pump" Carpenter. Besides C. B. Withington, there were Sylvanus D. Locke, also of Janesville, H. A. Holmes, of Beloit, John F. Appleby, of Mazomanie, W. W. Burson, Jacob Behel, George H. Spaulding, and Marquis L. Gorham, of Rockford.

Until 1880, all went well with McCormick and the Withington self-binder. Apparently, the process of invention had ceased. The Reaper had become of age. This miraculous wire-twisting machine was working everywhere with clock-like precision, and was believed to be the best that human ingenuity could devise. Then, like a bolt of lightning from a blue sky, came the news that William Deering had made and sold 3,000 *twine* self-binders, and that the farmers had all at once become prejudiced against the use of wire. Wire, they said, got mixed with the straw and killed their cattle. Wire fell in the wheat and made trouble in the flour-mills. Wire cut their hands. Wire cluttered up their barn-yards. They would have no more to do with wire. What they wanted and must have was *twine*.

William Deering, the newcomer who had caused this disturbance, became in a flash McCormick's ablest competitor. He had entered the business eight years before with a running start, having been a successful dry goods merchant in Maine. His geneology in the harvester industry shows that he had become an active partner of E. H. Gammon in 1872. Gammon, who had formerly been a Methodist preacher in Maine, had started as an agent for Seymour and Morgan of Brockport, which firm had been licensed by McCormick in 1845. Deering was the first highly skilled business man to enter the harvester trade. He was not a farmer's son, like McCormick. He was city-bred and factory trained. And in 1880 he staked practically his whole fortune upon the making of 3,000 twine self-binders, and won.

Cyrus McCormick saw at a glance that the wire self-binder must go. It was his policy to give the farmers what they wanted, rather than to force upon them an unpopular machine. So he called to his aid a mechanical genius named Marquis L. Gorham — one of those who had been lured into the quest of a self-binder by the insistence of "Pump" Carpenter. Gorham's most valuable contribution was a self-sizing device, by which all bound sheaves were made to be the same size. By the time that the grain stood ripe and yellow the following season, Gorham had prepared a twine self-binder that worked well, and McCormick, yielding to this sudden hostility against wire, pushed the Gorham machine with the full force of his great organization.

This evolution of the Reaper into the twine self-binder was a momentous event. It tremendously increased the sales. There were 60,000 machines of all kinds sold in 1880, and 250,000 in 1885 And it strikingly decreased the number of manufacturers. There were a hundred or more until the appearance of the twine binder: and all but twenty-two fell out of the race. Some of these were driven out by the expensive war of patents that now ensued. But most of them gave up the contest for lack of capital. The era of big production had arrived, and the little hand-labor shops could not produce an intricate self-binder for the low price at which they were being sold.

Even McCormick lost heavily at first, before a truce was called in this battle of the binders. One lawsuit cost him more than $225,000 and one experiment, with what was called a "low-down" binder, cost him $80,000. He was as determined as ever not to be beaten; and although he was at this time over seventy years of age, and sorely crippled by rheumatism, he straightway entered into a trade war with Deering, which was not ended until 1902. Many of the older workmen who are now employed in the McCormick works can remember the stress and strain of those battling years, and how their indomitable old leader, at times when he was unable to walk, would have himself pushed in a wheeled chair through the various buildings of his immense plant, to make sure that every part of the great mechanism was working smoothly.

Of all the competitors who had fought him in the early days, before the Civil War, there were few now remaining. Hussey, his first antagonist, had sold out to a mowing machine syndicate in 1861. Emerson, Seymour, and Morgan had decided not to make self-binders. Jerome Fassler, of Springfield, Ohio, took his fortune of two million dollars and went to New York City in 1882 with a scheme to build a subway. Manny was dead, and very few were living of those who had seen the Reaper of 1831.

John P. Adriance, of Poughkeepsie, had survived. He was a gentle-natured man, who was content with a small and safe percentage of the business. Byron E. Huntley, of Batavia, had also built up a small, but solidly based, enterprise. He had been the office-boy, in 1845, in the factory where the first hundred McCormick Reapers were made; and he had been a manufacturer on his own account since 1850. He, too, was a quiet, dignified man, very highly esteemed in both the United States and Europe. Lewis Miller, who deserves most credit as the creator of the mower, continued to do business at Akron. Mr. Miller was almost equally famous as a Methodist and the originator of the Chautauqua idea. At Auburn, N. Y., David M. Osborne was fighting manfully to keep in the race. He had built seven Reapers as early as 1856; and had made many friends by his ability and uprightness. At Hoosick Falls, N. Y., there was Walter A. Wood — a most competent and enterprising man; at Plano, Illinois, there was William H. Jones — self-made and as honest as the soil; and at Springfield, Ohio, were the picturesque William N. Whiteley and the powerful company of Warder, Bushnell, and Glessner. Whiteley was an inventor who had changed a McCormick Reaper into what he called a "combined machine"— a combined Reaper and mower. And Warder, Bushnell, and Glessner had begun to make McCormick Reapers, by means of a license from Seymour and Morgan, in 1852.

CYRUS HALL McCORMICK, 1858

Such were the most notable men who, together with McCormick and Deering, began
in 1880 or soon afterwards to manufacture the
new knot-tying device that had become necessary to the Reaper.   As for Cyrus H. McCormick himself, he lived to see it the universal
grain-cutter of all civilized countries.   He lived
to see it perfected into one of the most astonishing mechanisms known to man — an almost
rational machine that cuts the grain, carries it
on a canvas escalator up to steel hands that
shape it into bundles, tie a cord around it as
neatly as could be done by a sailor, and cut the
cord; after which the bound sheaf is pushed into
a basket and held until five of them have been
collected, whereupon they are dropped carefully
upon the ground.

Since 1884 there has been no essential change
in the fashion of the self-binder.   It is the same
to-day as when McCormick was alive.   In the
span of his single life the Reaper was born and
grew to its full maturity.   He saw its Alpha and
its Omega.   Best of all, he saw not only its
humble arrival, in a remote Virginia settlement,

but, as we shall see, he saw it become the play-
thing of Emperors, the marvel of Siberian plains-
men, the liberator of the land-serf in twenty
countries, and the bread-machine of one-half of
the human race.

CHAPTER VIII

THE CONQUEST OF EUROPE

BY 1850 Cyrus H. McCormick was ready for new business. He now had a factory of his own, and the assistance of his brothers, William and Leander. He had a score of busy agents and a few thousand dollars in the bank. He had fought down the ridicule of the farm-hands. It was only six years since he had set out from his Virginian farm with $300 in his belt and the Idea of the Reaper in his brain; but in those six years he had worked mightily and succeeded. His Reapers were now clicking merrily in more than three thousand American wheat-fields. So, it was a natural thing that in the first flush of victory, he should look across the sea for "more worlds to conquer."

There was at that time no general demand for Reapers in any European country. Labor was plentiful and cheap — forty cents a day in Great Britain and about half as much in Germany and France. In Austria and Russia the

farm laborers received no wages at all. They
were serfs. There was no economic reason why
serfs should be replaced by machinery. They
had first to become free and expensive to employ,
before this Reaper, this product of a free republic, could set them free from the drudgery
of the harvest.

England had been the first European country
to abolish this serfdom. Several centuries before, the ravages of the Black Death had made
farm laborers so scarce that their rights had
begun to be respected. Also, the upgrowth of
the factory system and the development of English shipping had called thousands of men away
from the fields, and raised the wages of those
who were left behind. And the falling off in
profits was compelling many English land-
owners to study better methods of farming, and
to favor the introduction of farm machinery.

Fortunately for McCormick, he had no sooner
begun to think of foreign trade than there came
the famous London Exposition of 1851. This
mammoth Exhibition was to Great Britain
what the Chicago World's Fair of 1893 was to

the United States — magnificent evidence of industrial progress. Its main promoter had been Prince Albert, the husband of Queen Victoria, and its success gave the keenest pleasure to the young Queen. In a letter written to the King of the Belgians, she thus describes her impressions upon the opening day:

"My dearest Uncle," she writes, "I wish you could have witnessed the 1st May, 1851, the *greatest* day in our history, the *most beautiful* and *imposing* and *touching* spectacle ever seen, and the triumph of my beloved Albert. Truly it was astonishing, a fairy scene. Many cried, and all felt touched and impressed with devotional feelings. It was the *happiest, proudest* day in my life, and I can think of nothing else. You will be astounded at this great work when you see it. The beauty of the building and the vastness of it all!"

The crowning jewel of this Exposition was the priceless Koh-i-noor diamond, which the Queen had received from India the previous year, and had loaned to the Exposition managers. For five thousand years, so the legend ran, this diamond had been one of the most precious treasures of Asia. It had been worn by the hero Karna. And it had been so often the most coveted prize in war that there was a Hindoo saying — "Whoever possesses the Koh-i-noor has conquered his enemies."

Most of the courts of Europe had sent some dazzling treasure. There were tapestries from the Viceroy of Egypt, and rugs from the Sultan of Turkey, and silks from the King of Spain. There were marbles from Paris, and paintings from Dresden, and embroideries from Vienna. And in the midst of this resplendent Exposition, surrounded and outshone by the exhibits of Russia, Austria, and France, lay a shabby collection of odds and ends from the United States.

For three weeks the American department was the joke of the Exposition. It was nicknamed the "Prairie Ground." It had no jewels, nor silks, nor golden candelabra. There were only such preposterous things as Dick's Press, Borden's Meat Biscuit, St. John's Soap, and McCormick's Reaper. This last contraption was the most preposterous of all. It was said to be "a cross between an Astley chariot, a wheelbarrow, and a flying-machine." It was unlike anything else that English eyes had ever seen, and by all odds the queerest and most ungainly thing that lay under the glass roof of the Crystal Palace. Undeniably it was the "Ugly Duckling" of the American exhibit.

But one day there came to the Reaper booth a remarkable Anglo-Italian named John J. Mechi. His father had been the barber of George III., and he himself, by the invention of a "Magic Razor Strop," had made a fortune. His hobby was scientific farming, and he was hungry for new methods and new ideas. At the time of the Exposition, his farm, which lay not far from London, had become the most famous experimental ground in England. Therefore, when he spied this new contrivance called a Reaper, he proposed that it be taken out to his farm and put to the test.

This was done on July twenty-fourth. In spite of a pouring rain, there were present a group of judges and two hundred farmers. Lord

Ebrington was there, and Prince Frederick of Holstein, and several other titled agriculturists. One other machine was to be tested, besides McCormick's. It was put into the grain first and was at once seen to be a failure. It broke down the grain instead of cutting it. Seeing this mishap, several of the farmers said to Mr. Mechi, "You had better stop this trial, because it is destroying your grain." Whereupon Mr. Mechi made one of the noblest replies that can be found in the annals of progress. "Gentlemen," he said, "this is a great experiment for the benefit of my country. When a new principle is about to be established, individual interests must always give way. If it is necessary for the success of this test, you may take my seventy acres of wheat."

Then came the McCormick Reaper, driven by an expert named Mackenzie. It swept down the field like a chariot of war, with whirling reel and clattering blade — seventy-four yards in seventy seconds. It was a miracle. Such a thing had never before been seen by Europeans. "This is a triumph for the American Reaper,"

said the delighted Mechi. "It has done its
work completely; and the day will come when
this machine will cut all the grain in England.
Now," he continued, swinging his hat, "let us,
as Englishmen, show our appreciation by giving three hearty English cheers."

Horace Greeley, who was present on this
occasion, described the victory of the McCormick
Reaper as follows: — "It came into the field
to confront a tribunal already prepared for its
condemnation. Before it stood John Bull —
burly, dogged, and determined not to be hum-
bugged, — his judgment made up and his sentence ready to be recorded. There was a moment, and but a moment, of suspense; then
human prejudice could hold out no longer;
and burst after burst of involuntary cheers from
the whole crowd proclaimed the triumph of the
Yankee Reaper. In seventy seconds McCormick had become famous. He was the lion of
the hour; and had he brought five hundred
Reapers with him, he could have sold them all."

Suddenly the "Ugly Duckling" had become
a swan. The glory of the Reaper began to

rival that of the Koh-i-noor. McCormick was
given not only a First Prize but a Council Medal,
such as was usually awarded only to Kings and
Governments. The London *Times*, which had
led the jeering, became now the loudest in the
chorus of approval. "The Reaping machine
from the United States," said the *Times* editor,
"is the most valuable contribution from abroad,
to the stock of our previous knowledge, that we
have yet discovered. It is worth the whole cost
of the Exposition." Also, speaking on behalf
of the English people, Sir Henry Lytton Bulwer
said, "For all manly and practical purposes, the
place of the United States is at the head of the
poll. Where, out of America, shall we get a
pistol like Mr. Colt's, to kill our eight enemies
in a second, or a reaping machine like Mr.
McCormick's, to clear out twenty acres of
wheat in a day?"

On the whole, this Exposition gave the United
States its first opportunity to answer the un-
pleasant questions that Sidney Smith had
asked in 1820. What have the Americans done,
he had asked, for the arts and sciences? Where

are their Arkwrights, their Watts, their Davys?
Here he was answered by the McCormick
Reaper, the Colt revolver, the Hobbs lock, the
Morse telegraph, the Howe sewing-machine,
the Deere plow, and the Hoe press. And, as
if to make the triumph of American invention
complete, it was in this year that the
yacht *America* easily out-classed the famous
yachts of England in a great race at Cowes,
and that the American steamer *Baltic*, of
the Collins Line, broke all the ocean records
and became the speediest vessel on the high seas.

This Exposition did much for McCormick.
It was the first appreciation of his work, in a
large way, that he had received. It was a welcome change after twenty strenuous years. It
gave him the distinction that a naturally strong
nature craved, and secured the friendship of
such eminent men as Junius Morgan, George
Peabody, J. J. Mechi, and Lord Granville.
From a business point of view, also, the Exposition was of great service to McCormick. It
enabled him to draw up a new plan of campaign for the foreign trade.

In the United States, he had made his appeal
directly to the mass of the farmers. In Europe
he could not do this. The vast bulk of the
farmers here were tenants or serfs. But it was
also true, he observed, that the Kings of Europe,
and the members of the nobility, were land-
owners. Here was his chance. He would be-
gin at the top. He would sell his Reapers to
the kings.

He noticed that kings and queens were not
the remote and inaccessible personages that he
had believed them to be. Prince Albert was
plainly more interested in farm machinery than
in the Koh-i-noor. The one prize which was
awarded to him personally was for a model
cottage, in which a workingman's family might
live with greater comfort. And one morning,
while McCormick was giving attention to his
Reaper, the Queen and her ten-year-old son
(now the King of England) walked past and
had a view of the American Reaping machine
that had been so widely ridiculed and praised.

McCormick had to hurry back to the United

States, on account of a patent suit that was then
in full swing; but before he left England he
established an agency in London, and started
a vigorous campaign among the titled land-
owners. He prepared a statement, showing
that even at the low rate of wages that were paid
on English farms a Reaper would mean a handsome saving to English wheat-growers. But he
did not depend upon the argument of economy.
He placed his reliance also upon the fact that
the Reaper had become the playtoy of kings,
and that their fancy would presently make it
the fashion.

Four years later he went with another Reaper
to an Exposition at Paris, won the Gold Medal,
and sold his machine to the Emperor. Then,
in 1862, with his wife and young son and
daughter, he made his headquarters in London,
and opened up a two-years' campaign in Great
Britain, Germany, and France. Up to this
time the foreign trade had grown but slowly.
All European countries combined were not buying more than half a million dollars' worth of

farm machinery a year from Americans — less than we sell them now in five days. So McCormick exerted himself to the utmost.

He held field tests to awaken the farmers. He advertised and organized. There were now several dozen other manufacturers in the field, all making Reapers more or less like McCormick's; and he gave battle to them at London, Lille, and Hamburg. After the Hamburg contest, Joseph A. Wright, the United States Commissioner, cabled to New York: "McCormick has thrashed all nations and walked off with the Gold Medal."

Again, in 1867, McCormick had a notable time at Paris. The Emperor Napoleon III., then in the last days of his inherited glory, permitted McCormick to give a sort of Reaper *matinée* on the royal estate at Châlons. The Emperor was present, at first on horseback, and then on foot. The sun was hot, and presently he said to McCormick, "If you will allow me, I'll come under your umbrella." So the two men, dramatically different in the tendencies they represented, walked arm in arm behind the Reaper, and watched it automatically cut and rake off the grain. The Emperor was delighted. He forgot for the moment his impending troubles, and at once offered McCormick the Cross of the Legion of Honor. This was, in all probability, the last time that the coveted Cross was conferred in France by the hand of a sovereign; and the meeting of the two men was a highly impressive event, the one man typifying a falling dynasty that had risen to greatness by the sword, and the other the founder of a new industry that was destined to bring peace and plenty to all nations alike.

Two years later, because of the clamor of McCormick's competitors, a grand Field Test was arranged by the German Government at Altenberg. Thirty-eight contestants entered the lists, and after a most exciting tournament the judges awarded the Gold Medal and a special prize of sixty ducats to McCormick. Such contests, from this time onward, came thick and fast. Several days later McCormick swept the field at Altona. In 1873 he was decorated by the Austrian Emperor. And in

1878 the French Academy of Science elected him a member, for the reason that he "had done more for the cause of agriculture than any other living man."

From that time to the present day the making of Reapers and Harvesters has remained an American business. An American machine must pay twenty dollars to enter France, and twenty-five to enter Hungary. But try as they may, other nations cannot learn the secret of the Reaper. They cannot produce a machine that is at once so complex, so hardy, and so efficient. When Bismarck, at the close of his life, was inspecting several American self-binders which he had bought for his farm at Fredericksruhe, he asked, "Why do they not make these machines in Germany?" As we have seen, had he wished a complete answer he would have had to read the history of the United States. He would have seen that the Reaper can be produced only in countries where labor receives a high reward, where farmers own their own acres without fear of being despoiled by invading armies, and where the

CYRUS HALL McCORMICK, 1867

From Painting by Cabanel

average of intelligence and enterprise is as high in the country as in the city.

In 1898 Europe had become so dependent upon America for its reaping machinery that 22,000 machines were shipped from the McCormick plant alone — so many that a fleet of twelve vessels had to be chartered to carry them. There are now as many American Reapers and Harvesters in Europe as can do the work of 12,000,000 men. Of all American machines exported, the Reaper is at the head of the list. It has been the chief pathfinder for our foreign trade. Four-fifths of all the harvesting machinery in the world is made in the United States; and one-third, perhaps more, in the immense factory-city that Cyrus H. McCormick founded in Chicago in 1847.

It was McCormick's most solid satisfaction, in his later life, to see foreign nations, one by one, adopt his invention and move up out of the Famine Zone. No news was at any time more welcome to him than the tidings that a new territory had been entered. And although the foreign trade has been vastly multiplied in

the past five or six years, he lived long enough to
see his catalogue printed in twenty languages,
and to know that as long as the human race
continued to eat bread, the sun would never
set upon the empire of the Reaper.

CHAPTER IX

McCORMICK AS A MANUFACTURER

"IF I had given up business, I would have been dead long ago," said Cyrus H. McCormick in 1884, only a few weeks before his death; and this statement was by no means an exaggeration. His business was his life. It was not a definite, walled-off fraction of his life, as with most men. It was the whole of it. His business was his work, his play, his religion, his grand opera, his education. There was business even in his love-letters and his dreams.

McCormick believed in business. He had the sturdy pride of a "John Halifax, Gentleman." He never wanted to be anything else but a worker. He never wasted a breath in wishing for an easier life. He worked hard for twenty-five years after he had made his fortune, because he believed in work and commerce and the reciprocities of trade. He was never dazzled nor deflected for a moment by the pomps and pageantries of the world, and for the glory that springs from war he had very little respect.   In 1847, when offering a place in his factory to his brother Leander, he writes, "This will be as honorable an enterprise as to go to Mexico to be shot at."   And in later life, in a conversation with General Lilley, of Virginia, he said, "I expect to die in the harness, because this is not the world for rest.   This is the world for work. In the next world we will have the rest."

In the vast mass of letters, papers, etc., left by Mr. McCormick, there is one mention, and only one, of recreation.   After his first visit to the West, in 1844, he wrote to one of his brothers and described a hunting trip in which he shot three prairie chickens near Beloit.   But during the rest of his life, he was too busy for sport. His energy was the wonder of his friends and the despair of his employees.   His brain was not quick.   It was not marvellously keen nor marvellously intuitive.   But it was at work every waking moment, like a great engine that never tires.

"He was the most laborious worker I ever saw," said one of his secretaries.   One of the

words that annoyed him most was *to-morrow.*
He wanted things done to-day. With regard
to every important piece of work, it was his
instinct to "do it now." He abhorred delay
and dawdling. Even as a boy, when sent on
an errand, he would set off upon a run. Walking was too slow. And although he was in
France on many occasions, the French phrase
that he knew best was *"Depechez-vous."*

His plan of work, so far as he could be said
to have a plan, was this — *One Thing at a Time,
and the Hardest Thing First.* He followed the
line of *most* resistance. If the hardest thing
can be done, he reasoned, all the rest will follow.
And as for all work that was merely routine,
he left as much as possible of it to others.

He was not an organizer so much as a creator
and a pioneer. His problem was not like that
which troubles the business men of to-day. He
was not grappling with the evils of competition,
nor with the higher questions of efficiency and
"community of interest." He was making a
business that had not existed. He was clearing
away obstacles that are now wholly forgotten.

Consequently, as each new difficulty appeared, he had to consider it in all its details. He could not pass it over to Lieutenant Number One or Lieutenant Number Two.

McCormick was like a general who was leading an army into an unknown country rather than like the business man of the twentieth century, who can travel by time-table and schedule. When an obstacle blocked his path, it had to be removed; and until it was out of the way, nothing else mattered. Thus it was impossible for McCormick to have business hours. Once his mind had applied itself to a problem, he cared nothing for clocks and watches. Sometimes he would work on through the night, hour after hour, until the gray light of another day shone in the window. On all these arduous occasions, he had no idea of time, and he would allow no distractions nor interruptions. So rigid was this grasp of his mind that if his body rebelled and he fell asleep, he would invariably when he woke take up the matter in hand at the exact point at which it had been left. Not even

sleep could detach his mind from a task that
was unfinished.

When anything was going well, he let it alone.
As soon as his factory was in good running order,
he gave it little attention.   It was managed first
by his brothers, William and Leander, and
afterwards by such thoroughly competent men
as Charles Spring and E. K. Butler.   The work
that he chose to do himself was invariably new
business. He cared little for the mere making
of money. The success always pleased him
much more than the profit. He was at heart
a builder, and therefore when he had finished
one structure, he moved off and began another.

It is a remarkable fact that as an investor,
also, he had no interest in businesses that were
already established.   Stocks were offered to him,
stocks that were safe and sure, but he bought
none of them.   The money that he invested outside of his own business was put into pioneering
enterprises. He bought land in Chicago and
Arizona. He opened up gold mines in South
Carolina and Montana.   He supplied the capital

for a company which set out to bring mahogany from San Domingo. He invested $55,000 in the Tehuantepec Inter-Ocean Railroad, an ambitious attempt to join the Atlantic and Pacific oceans by rail, which was begun in 1879 and came to an inglorious end several years later. And he was one of that daring group of Americans who planned and financed the Union Pacific Railway — the first road that really joined sea to sea and reached to the farthest acre in the West.

In all these undertakings he lost money, except in the instances of Chicago real estate and the Union Pacific. By 1883 he had several hundred thousand dollars invested in gold mines, and yet had not received one dollar of profit. It was the fascination of pioneering that had lured him. He saw no charm, as the gambler does, in the risk itself. The Wall Street game he regarded as child's play. The thing that gripped him was the developing of new material resources — the colonization of new lands — the mastery of whatever is hostile to the welfare of the human race.

McCORMICK REAPER CUTTING ON A SIDE HILL IN PENNSYLVANIA

Another McCormick trait, which is not usually found in men who have the pioneering instinct, was *Thoroughness*. He never said, "This is good enough," or "Half a loaf is better than no bread." He wanted what was *right* whether it came to him or went from him. He never believed in a ninety per cent success. He wanted par. Once his mind was fully aroused upon a subject, there was no detail too petty for him to consider. He labored hard to be correct in matters that appeared trifling to other men. Even in his letters to members of his family, the sentences were carefully formed, and there were no misspelled words. Once he gave advice to a younger brother on the importance of spelling words correctly. "You should carry a dictionary, as I do," he said.

All slovenliness, whether of mind or body, he abhorred. To take thought about a matter and to do it as it ought to be done, was to him a matter of character as well as of business. When a telegram was submitted to him for approval, it was his custom to draw a circle around the superfluous words. This was a

little lesson to his managers on the importance
of brevity and exactness. He insisted that clocks
and watches should be correct, and in his later
life carried a fine repeater which could strike
the hour in the night and in which he took an
almost boyish pride. Once, when he had been
given the management of a political campaign
in Chicago, he created consternation among
the politicians by the rigid way in which he
supervised the expense accounts. "This will
never do," he said. "Things are at loose ends."
If a bill was ten cents too much it went back.
One bill for $15 was held up for a week be-
cause it was not properly drawn. The amazed
politicians could not understand such a man,
— who would readily sign a check for $10,-
000, and put it in the campaign treasury, and
yet make trouble about the misplacing of a
dime of other people's money.

McCormick demanded absolute honesty from
his employees. One young man lost his chance
of promotion because he was seen to place a
two-cent stamp, belonging to the firm, on one
of his personal letters. But once he had tested

a man, and found him to be pure gold, he trusted him completely. A new employee would be pelted with questions and complete answers insisted upon. This was often a harsh ordeal. It was irritating to a man of independent spirit, until he realized that it was a sort of discipline and examination.

McCormick was always an optimist. He was not one of those who said, "Let well enough alone."

He never endured unsatisfactory business conditions. When he found that the freight charges on Reapers from Virginia to Cincinnati were too high, he arranged to have Reapers built in Cincinnati. When he found that other manufacturers were apt to be careless as to the quality of their materials, he built a factory of his own. Again and again in the course of his life, came the temptation to be satisfied with what he had already achieved. But he could not endure the thought of being beaten. Instead of being content and complacent, he was far more likely to be planning a wholly new policy, on larger lines.

A daring proposition from a competent man always caught his attention. Once, when he was sitting in his office, he heard E. K. Butler, who was at that time the head of his sales department, protest that the factory was not making as many machines as it should. "It is sheer nonsense," said Butler, "to say that the factory is producing as much as it can. If I were at the head of it, I could double the output with very little extra expense." Most employers would have regarded this sort of talk as mere boastfulness, but not so McCormick. He knew that Butler was a most adaptable and competent man, so he called him into the office and straightway appointed him to be the superintendent of the factory. Butler was thus put upon his mettle. He went out to the factory resolved that McCormick's confidence in him should not be overthrown. He routed the wastes and inefficiencies, and keyed the whole plant up to such a pitch that, in a remarkably short period, he had made good his boast and doubled the output without hiring an extra man.

But the preëminent quality in the character

of Cyrus McCormick was not his power of concentration, nor his spirit of pioneering, nor his thoroughness. It was his strength of will — his *Tenacity*. This was the motif of his life.

He was not at all a shrewd accumulator of millions, as many have imagined him. He had not an iota of craft and cunning. Neither was he a financier, in the modern sense. It would be nearer the truth to say that he was a farmer-manufacturer, of simple nature but tremendous resolution, whose one overmastering life-purpose was to teach the wheat nations of the world to use his harvesting machinery.

"The exhibition of his powerful will was at times actually terrible," said one of his lawyers. "If any other man on this earth ever had such a will, certainly I have not heard of it."

A drizzle of little annoyances and little matters always irritated him, but he could stand up alone against a sea of adversity without a whimper. In fact, he would sooner be asked for a thousand dollars than for fifty cents. He would storm over the loss of a carpet slipper and smile blandly at the loss of a lawsuit. "He made more fuss over a pin-prick," said one of his valets, "than he did over a surgical operation." He disliked the petty odds and ends of life. His mind was too massive to adapt itself readily to small matters. But when a great difficulty came in view, he rose and went at it with a sort of stern satisfaction and religious zeal. He was so confident of his own strength, and of the justice of his cause, that it was almost a joy to him to —

> " Breast the blows of circumstance,
> And grasp the skirts of happy chance,
> And grapple with his evil star."

A defeat never meant anything more to McCormick than a delay. Often, the harder he was thrown down the higher he would rebound. Again and again he was thwarted and blocked. In the race of competition, there was a time when he was beaten by Whiteley, and there was a time when he was beaten by Deering. Most of his lawsuits were decided against him. But no one ever saw him crushed or really disheartened. In 1877, after he had made a long hard struggle to become a United States Senator,

the news came to him that he was defeated.
"Well," he said, "that's over. What next?"

Usually, McCormick was at his best when
the situation was at its worst. His Titanic work
immediately after the great Chicago Fire of 1871
is the most striking evidence of this. He had
been living at the corner of Tenth Street and
Fifth Avenue, in New York City, for four years
before the Fire; but he was in Chicago during
the greatest of all Illinois disasters. In one day
of fire and terror he saw his city reduced to a
waste of ashes. It was no longer a city. It
was two thousand acres of desolation. He was
himself in the midst of the fire-fighting. When
his wife, in response to his telegraphic message,
came to him in Chicago two days later, he met
her wearing a half-burned hat and a half-
burned overcoat. His big factory, which was at
that time making about 10,000 harvesters a
year, was wholly destroyed. In a flash he found
himself without a city and without a business.

But McCormick never flinched. The arrival
of a great difficulty was always his cue. First
he ascertained his wife's wishes. Did she wish

the factory to be rebuilt, or did she want him to retire from active business life? She, thinking of her son, said — "Rebuild." At once McCormick became the most buoyant and confident citizen in the ruined city. His great spirit was aroused. He called up one of his attorneys and sent him in haste to the docks to buy lumber. He telegraphed to his agents to rush in as much money as they could collect. Every bank in the city had been burned, so for a time this money was kept by the cashier in a market basket, and carried at night to a private house. There was one day as much as $24,000 in the basket. Before the cinders were cool, McCormick had given orders to build a new factory, larger than the one that had been burned down. More than this, he had also given orders that his house in New York should be sold, and that a home should be established in Chicago. Chicago was his city. He had seen it grow from 10,000 to 325,000. And in this hour of its distress he tossed aside all other plans and gave Chicago all he had.

His unconquerableness gave heart to others.

Several of the wealthiest citizens, who had lost courage, rallied to the help of the city. One merchant, who had lost his store, borrowed $100,000 from McCormick and started again. And so McCormick became not only one of the main builders of the first Chicago, but also of the second Chicago, which in less than three years had become larger and finer than the city that was.

It was this steel-fibred tenacity that was the main factor in the success of McCormick, whether we consider him as a manufacturer or as a great American. It enabled him to establish the perilous industry of making harvesting machines — a business so complex and many-sided that out of every twenty manufacturers who set out to emulate McCormick, only one survives today. It enabled McCormick to hold his own in spite of adverse litigation, the hostility of Congress, the rivalry of other inventors, and the calamity of the Great Fire. It was so remarkable, and so productive of good to his country and to himself, that he will always remain one of the creative and heroic figures in the early industrial history of the United States.

CHAPTER X

CYRUS H. McCORMICK was a great
commercial Thor. He was six feet tall,
weighed two hundred pounds, and had the
massive shoulders of a wrestler. His body was
well proportioned, with small hands and feet.
His hair, even in old age, was very dark and
waving. His bearing was erect, his manner
often imperious, and his general appearance
that of a man built on large lines and for
large affairs.

Men of lesser caliber regarded him with fear,
not for any definite reason, but because, as
Seneca has said — "In him that has power, all
men consider not what he has done, but what
he may do." He was so strong, so dominating,
so ready to crash through obstacles by sheer bulk
of will-power, that smaller men could never quite
subdue a feeling of alarm while they were in
his presence. He was impatient of small talk
and small criticisms and small objections. He

had no tact at retail, and he saw no differences in little-minded people. All his life he had been plagued and obstructed by the Liliputians of the world, and he had no patience to listen to their chattering. He was often as rude as Carlyle to those who tied their little threads of pessimism across his path.

At fashionable gatherings he would now and then be seen — a dignified figure; but his mind was almost too ponderous an engine to do good service in a light conversation. If a subject did not interest him, he had nothing to say. What gave him, perhaps, the highest degree of social pleasure, was the entertaining, at his house, of such men as Horace Greeley, William H. Seward, Peter Cooper, Abram S. Hewitt, George Peabody, Junius Morgan, Cyrus W. Field, or some old friend from Virginia.

His long years of pioneering had made him a self-sufficient man, and a man who lived from within. He did not pick up his opinions on the streets. His mind was not open to any chance idea. He had certain clear, definite convictions, logical and consistent. What he knew, he knew. There were no hazy imaginings in his mind. The main secret of his power lay in his ability to focus all his energies upon a few subjects. Once, in 1848, he mentioned the French Revolution in one of his letters. "It is a mighty affair," he wrote, "and will be likely to stand." But usually he paid little attention to the world-dramas that were being enacted. He was too busy — too devoted to affairs which, if he did not attend to them, would not be attended to at all.

McCormick was a product of the Protestant Reformation, and of the capitalistic development that came with it. The whole structure of his character was based upon the two great dogmas of the Reformation — the sovereignty of God and the direct responsibility of the individual. Whoever would know the springs at which his life was fed must read the story of Luther, Calvin, and Knox. They must call to mind the attitude of Luther at the Diet of Worms, when he faced the men who had the power to take his life and said, "Here I stand.

I can do no other." They must recollect how these three men, who were leaders of nations, not sects, stood out alone against the kings and ecclesiasticisms of Europe, without wealth, without armies, without anything except a higher Moral Idea, and succeeded so mightily they actually changed the course of empires and became the pathfinders of the human race.

McCormick was so essentially a result of this religio-economic movement that it is impossible to separate his religion and his business life. He was an individualist through and through — as well marked a type of the Covenanter in commerce as the United States has ever produced. He believed in presbyters in religion, private capitalists in business, and elected representatives in government. He was opposed to feudalism and bureaucracy in all their myriad forms. He held the middle ground, the *via media*, between the over-organization of the fourteenth century, when the rights of the individual were forgotten, and the lax liberalism of to-day, when too much is left to individual whim and caprice, and when duties and responsibilities are too apt to be ignored.

Above all constituted authorities stood a man's own conscience. This was McCormick's faith, and it was this that made him the fighter that he was. It gave him courage and the fortitude that is rarer than courage. It compelled him to oppose his own political party at the Baltimore Convention of 1861. It made him stand single-handed against his fellow-manufacturers, in defence of his rights as an inventor. It enabled him to beat down the Pennsylvania Railroad, after a twenty-three year contest, and to prove that a great corporation cannot lawfully do an injustice to an individual.

McCormick was nourished on this virile Calvinistic faith from the time when he first learned to read out of the Shorter Catechism and the Bible. It had been the faith of his fathers for generations, and it was bred into him from boyhood. Nevertheless, according to the practice of the Presbyterians, there had to come a time when he himself openly made his choice. This

occasion came in 1834, when McCormick was
twenty-five years of age. A four-day meeting
was being held in the little stone church on his
grandfather's farm.   Three ministers were in
charge.   As was the custom, there was constant
preaching from morning until sundown, with
an hour's respite for dinner. At the close of
the fourth day, all who wished to become avowed
Christians were requested to stand up.   Cyrus
McCormick was there, and he was not a member
of the church; yet he did not stand up.   That
night his father went to his bedside and gently
reproached him.   "My son," he said, "don't
you know that your silence is a public rejection
of your Saviour?" Cyrus was conscience-
stricken.   He leapt from his bed and began to
dress himself.   "I'll go and see old Billy Mc-
Clung," he said.   Half an hour later, old Billy
McClung, who was a universally respected religious leader in the community, was amazed to
be called out of his sleep by a greatly troubled
young man, who wanted to know by what means
he might make his peace with his Maker.   The
next Sunday this young man stood up in the

church, and became in name what he already was by nature and inheritance — a Christian of the Presbyterian faith.

After he left home his letters to the members of his family are strewn with scraps of religious reflection. In 1845, for instance, he writes, "Business is not inconsistent with Christianity; but the latter ought to be a help to the former, giving a confidence and resignation, after using all proper means; and yet I have sometimes felt that I came so far short of the right *feeling*, so worldly-minded, that I could wish myself out of the world." On another occasion, when he was struggling with manufacturers who had broken their contracts, he wrote, "If it were not for the fact that Providence has seemed to assist me in our business, it has at times seemed that I would almost sink under the weight of responsibility hanging upon me; but I believe the Lord will help us out." And after his first visit to New York City, he summed up his impressions of the metropolis in the following sentence, "It is a desirable place and people, with regular and good Presbyterian preaching."

McCormick enjoyed with all his heart the logical, doctrinal sermon. His favorite Bible passage was the eighth chapter of Romans, that indomitable victorious chapter that ends like the blast of a trumpet:

"Who shall separate us from the love of Christ? Shall tribulation, or distress, or persecution, or famine, or nakedness, or peril, or sword? As it is written, 'for Thy sake we are killed all the day long; we are accounted as sheep for the slaughter.' Nay, in all these things we are more than conquerors through Him that loved us; for I am persuaded that neither death, nor life, nor angels, nor principalities, nor powers, nor things present, nor things to come, nor height, nor depth, nor any other creature, shall be able to separate us from the love of God, which is in Christ Jesus, our Lord."

His favorite hymn, which he sang often and with the deepest fervor, was that melodious prayer that begins —

"O Thou in whose presence my soul takes delight,
  On whom in affliction I call,
· My comfort by day, and my song in the night,
  My hope, my salvation, my all."

In his earlier journeys through the Middle
West, McCormick was distressed at the rough
immorality of the new settlements. "I see a
great deal of profanity and infidelity in this
country, enough to make the heart sick," he
wrote in 1845. These towns and villages needed
more preachers, and better preachers, he thought.
Consequently, soon after he had acquired his
first million dollars, he determined to establish
the best possible college for the education of
ministers. He almost stunned with joy the
Western friends of higher education for ministers,
by offering them $100,000 with which to estab-
lish a school of theology in Chicago. This offer
was made in 1859 — half a century ago, and
resulted in the removal of a moneyless and de-
caying Seminary at New Albany, Indiana, to
Chicago. Thus was founded the Northwestern
Theological Seminary, afterwards named the
McCormick Theological Seminary, which, in
its fifty years of life, has given a Christian education to thousands of young men.

Thirteen years later he bought *The Interior*
and made it what it has remained ever since —

a religious weekly of the highest rank. These two — the college and the paper — were his pride and delight. He fathered them in the most affectionate way. No matter what crisis might be impending in the war of business, he always had time to talk to his editors and his professors. So, though McCormick had received much from his religious inheritance, it is also true that he gave back much. His last public speech, which was read for him by his son Cyrus because he was too weak to deliver it himself, was given at the laying of the corner-stone of a new building which he had given to the college. Its last sentence was typical of McCormick — full of hope and optimism: "I never doubted that success would ultimately reward our efforts," he said; "and now, on this occasion, we may fairly say that the night has given place to the dawn of a brighter day than any which has hitherto shone upon us."

McCormick went into politics, too, with the same conscientious abandon with which he plunged into business and religion. He was a Democrat of the Jeffersonian type. One of his

keenest pleasures was to go to the Senate and
listen to its debates.   He was not a fluent speaker
himself, but he delighted in the orations of Clay,
Calhoun, and Webster.   He believed in politics.
He thought it a public danger that the strong
and competent men of the republic should will-
ingly permit men of little ability and low character to manage public affairs.   In fact, he was
almost as much a pathfinder and pioneer in this
matter as he had been in matters of business,
but without the same measure of success.   Politics, he found, was not like business.   Its
successes depended not upon your own efforts,
but upon the votes of the majority.

What McCormick tried to do as a citizen and
a patriot was the one heroic failure of his life.
He ran for office on several occasions, but he
was never elected.   He was not the sort of man
who gets elected.   He stood for his whole party
at a time when the average politician was standing only for himself.   He talked of "fundamental principles" while the other leaders, for the
most part, were thinking of salaries.   He gave
up his time and his money as freely for politics

as he did for religion; but he was out of his
element.   He was too sincere, too simple, too
intent upon a larger view of public questions.
He could never talk the flexible language of
diplomacy nor suit his theme to the prejudice
of his listeners.   Usually, to the political managers and delegates with whom he felt it his
duty to co-operate, he was like a man from
another world.   They could never understand
him, and tolerated his leadership mainly because of his generous contributions.   Again and
again he astonished them by developing a party
speech into a sermon on national righteousness,
or by speaking nobly of a political opponent.
On one memorable occasion, for instance, in
the white-hot passion of the Hayes-Tilden con-
troversy, and after he had lavished time and
money in support of Tilden, he sprang to his
feet in a Democratic convention and amazed
the delegates by saying: "Mr. Hayes is not a
Democrat, but he is too patriotic and honest
to suit his party managers and we must sustain
him so far as he is right."

He was one of the first Americans who rose

[165]

above sectional interests and party loyalties, and surveyed his country as a whole. No other man of his day, either in or out of public office, was so free from local prejudices and so intensely national in his beliefs and sympathies. He refused to stamp himself with the label of the North or of the South. He had been reared in the one and matured in the other. And in the ominous days before the Civil War he strove like a beneficent giant to make the wrangling partisans listen to the voice of reason and arbitration.

He went to the Democratic Convention at Baltimore, just before the war, and set before the Southerners the standpoint of the North. Then he bought a daily paper — *The Times* — to explain to Chicago the standpoint of the South. He wrote editorials. He made speeches. He poured into the newspapers, day after day for two years, a large share of the profits that he derived from his Reaper. He was no more popular as an editor than as a political candidate. He was a maker, not a collector, of public opinion; and instead of pandering to the war

THE REAPER IN HEAVY GRAIN

frenzy, he opposed it, — put his newspaper squarely in its path, and held it there until the feet of the crowd had trampled it into an impossible wreck.

He was so strong, so indomitable, this heir of the Covenanters, that when the war had openly begun, he strode between the North and South and labored like a Titan to bring them to a reconciliation. He actually believed that he could establish peace. He proposed a plan. Horace Greeley indorsed it, and the two men, who were throughout life the closest of comrades, undertook to bring the severed nation back to union and the paths of law.

The "McCormick Plan," in a word was to call immediately two conventions — one to represent the Democrats of the North and the other the Democrats of the South. These conventions would elect delegates to a board of arbitration, which would consider the various causes of the war and arrange a just basis upon which both sides could agree to disband their armies and reëstablish peace.

After the war, too, almost before the nation

had finished counting its dead, it was Cyrus H. McCormick whose voice was first heard in favor of church unity. Among the many speeches and letters of his which have been preserved, the most beautifully phrased paragraph is the ending of an article that he published in 1869, protesting against the invasion of political partisanism into the religious life.

"When are we to look for the return of brotherly love and Christian fellowship," he asked, "so long as those who aspire to fill the high places of the church indulge in such wrath and bitterness? Now that the great conflict of the Civil War is past, and its issues settled, religion and patriotism alike require the exercise of mutual forbearance, and the pursuit of those things which tend to peace."

For the mere game of party politics Mr. McCormick cared little or nothing. It was all as irksome to him as the task of governing Geneva was to John Calvin; but he could not help himself. His political convictions were bone of his bone and flesh of his flesh. They were racial traits which his forefathers and foremothers had spent at least three centuries in developing.

On one occasion Dr. John Hall of New York, seeing how Mr. McCormick was worried by political obligations, said to him:

"Why do you plague yourself with these uncongenial things? What glory can you hope to get from politics that will add to what you now possess as the inventor of the Reaper?"

"Dr. Hall," replied Mr. McCormick, "I am in politics because I cannot help it. There are certain principles that I have got to stand by, and I am obliged to go into politics to defend them."

The form of Mr. McCormick's religious faith had been forged by such preacher-patriots as John Knox and Andrew Melville; and he, like them, found it as imperative upon his conscience to fight for both civil and religious liberty. With his whole heart he believed in American institutions as they had been established by the nation-builders of 1776. He did not want the Constitution to be ignored by Federal reformers, nor the Union to be broken by secession. He was by temperament and tradition a conservative, and opposed especially to all extreme measures and sectional innovations. As he had adapted his Reaper so that it would cut grain in all States, he could never see why political policies, too, should not be lifted above the limitations of geography and made to conserve the welfare of the whole people. As he said on one strenuous occasion when laboring mightily to beat back the extremists in his own party: "Is not every government on the face of the earth established upon the principle of compromise?"

To special privileges of every sort he was unalterably opposed. He asked for none for himself — no favoring tariff or grant of public land or monopolistic franchise. "I have been throughout my life," he said, "opposed to all measures which tend to raise one class of the American people upon the ruin of others, or one section of our common country at the expense of another. The country is the common property of all parties, and all are interested in its prosperity."

All this shows the heroic side of McCormick; but he was not always heroic. He was a giant, but a most human and simple-natured giant. Strange as it may sound to those who knew him only with his armor on, it is true that he could be tender or humorous. There were tears and laughter in him, There was no cruelty in his strength and no revenge in his aggressiveness. He was a big, red-blooded, great-hearted man, who might to-day be threatening to cane a politician who had deceived him, and to-morrow be playing with his younger children and letting their two pet squirrels, Zip and Zoe, chase each other around his shoulders.

He was fond of power, not because of its privileges and exemptions, but because it furthered the work that he had in hand. He was often surrounded by sycophants — by men who said yes to his yes and no to his no; and while he accepted this homage with a certain degree of satisfaction, he was not deceived by it. On one occasion, when he was attending the Democratic Convention at Cincinnati — the convention that nominated Hancock as candidate for President,— he was beset by a court of flatterers and lip-servers. After it was over, he remarked simply to his valet, "Well, Charlie, there is a lot of farce and humbug about this."

Dr. Francis L. Patton, who was for years the president of Princeton University and also at one time editor of *The Interior*, was especially impressed with this direct naturalness of Mc-Cormick. "One meets with all sorts of men in the course of a lifetime," said Dr. Patton. "There are patronizing men, pompous men, men who habitually wear a mask of seriousness, men who clothe themselves with dignity as with a coat of mail lest you should presume too much or go too far, men whose position is never defined, and double-minded men with whom you never feel yourself safe. But Mr. Mc-Cormick was not like one of these. There is that in the possession of power which always tends to make men imperious. I do not mean to imply that he was altogether free from this tendency, for he was not. But he was approach-able, companionable, and ready to hear what I had to say. He was not one of those men who are so uninterestingly self-controlled as to be always the same. There were times when his mirth was contagious and times when his wrath was kindled a little. We did not always agree, and sometimes we both grew hot in argument; but at the end his cheery laugh proclaimed the fact that our differences had only been the free and easy give-and-take of friendship."

To see McCormick laugh was a spectacle. There was first a mellowing of his usual Jovian manner. His gray-brown eyes twinkled. The tense lines of his face relaxed. Then came a smile and soon a burst of laughter, shaking his powerful body and putting the whole company for the time into an uproar of merriment. It was the triumph of the genial and magnetic side of his nature — the side that was ordinarily repressed by the pressure of his big affairs.

McCormick had humor, but not wit. His jokes were simple and old-fashioned, such as Luther and Cromwell would have laughed at. There was no innuendo and no cynicism. On one occasion two small urchins knocked at

the door and asked for food. McCormick heard
their voices and had them brought into the sit-
ting-room, where he happened to be in con-
sultation with his lawyer. "Now," said he to
the youngsters, "we are going to put both of you
on trial. I will be the judge and this gentleman will be the prosecutor." Each boy in
turn was placed on the witness-stand, and plied
with questions. It was soon clear that neither
of them was telling the truth, so "Judge" Mc-
Cormick took them in hand and gave them a
serious talk on the folly and wickedness of lying.
Then he gave them twenty-five cents apiece,
and sent them down to the kitchen to eat as
much supper as they could hold.

At another time a very dignified and self-
centred military officer was taking supper with
the McCormick family. The first course, as
usual, was corn-meal mush and milk. This
was served in Scotch fashion, with the hot mush
in one bowl and the cold milk in another, and
the practice was to so co-ordinate the eating of
these that both were finished at the same time.
The officer planned his spoonfuls badly, and

HARVESTING NEAR SPOKANE, WASHINGTON

was soon out of milk. "Have some more milk to finish your mush, Colonel," said McCormick. Several minutes later the Colonel's mush bowl was empty, at which McCormick said, "Have some more mush to finish your milk." And so it went, with milk for the mush and mush for the milk, until the unfortunate Colonel was hopelessly incapacitated for the four or five courses that came afterwards.

McCormick was not by any means a teller of stories, but he had a few simple and well-worn anecdotes that appealed so strongly to his sense of humor that he told and re-told them many times. There was the story of the man who stole the pound of butter and hid it in his hat, and how the grocer saw him and kept talking in the store, beside a hot stove, until the butter melted and exposed the man's thievery. Another favorite story was about the pig that found its way into a garden by walking through a hollow log, and how the gardener fooled the pig by placing the hollow log in such a way that both ends of it were on the outside of the garden.

Even McCormick's jokes had a certain moral tang — a flavor of the first Psalm and the eighth chapter of Romans. They were apt to deal with the troubles of the ungodly who had been caught in their wickedness. There were times, too, when his sense of humor and his sense of justice would co-operate in odd ways. Once, when a roast game bird, which had been sent to him as a gift from the hunter, was left over from supper, he ordered that his dainty be kept and served for the next day's luncheon. At luncheon the next day it did not appear. On asking for the game bird, a roast chicken was set before him, and he at once noticed that it was not the same bird which he had ordered to be kept. He questioned the butler, who protested that it was the same. After the meal McCormick ordered that the servants involved should be called into the dining-room. From them, by a series of questions, he soon obtained the truth and proved the butler to be the culprit. The one thing that he would tolerate least was a lie. As he would say at times, "A thief you can watch, but I detest a liar."

There were very few who had the temerity to
play a practical joke upon the great inventor
himself. His two youngest sons, Harold and
Stanley, would hide in the hallway when they
saw him approaching, and pounce out upon
him with wild yells in small-boy fashion, but
they were both privileged people.

McCormick was a most hearty and hospitable
man. He was an ideal person for such a life-
work — the abolition of famine. He was fond
of food and plenty of it. He loved to see a big
table heaped with food. The idea of hunger was
intolerable to him. He might well have been
posing for a statue of the deity of Plenty, as he
squared himself around to the long, family
dinner-table, with his napkin worn high and
caught at his shoulders by a white silk band that
went around his neck, and with a complacent,
"Now, then," plunged the carving-fork into a
crisp and fragrant fowl that lay on the platter
in front of him.

The fact that McCormick seldom made a
social call was not due to his own choosing, but
because of the many worries and compulsions

of his life. Once, when confiding in an intimate friend, he said, "It pains me very much to think how little I am known by my neighbors, but I seem to be always too busy to meet them." He was not at all, as many have thought because of his strenuous life, a man of harsh and rough exterior. There was nothing rough about him except his strength. He was irreproachable in dress and personal appearance. He did not drink, smoke, nor swear. And his manners and language, on formal occasions, were those of a dignified gentleman of the old school — a Calhoun, or a Van Buren.

He was not a hard-natured man, except when he was battling for his rights and his principles. He would often turn from an overwhelming mass of business to play with one of his children. He was as ready to forgive as he was to fight. He never cherished resentments or personal grudges. He knew that life was a conflict of interests and policies; and when he forgave, his forgiveness was free and full, and not a formal ceremony. It was as honest and as spontaneous as his wrath. He was one of the few men who could freely

pray, "Forgive us our trespasses as we forgive
those who trespass against us."

His fame and honors and intimacies with
people of rank never made him less democratic
in his sympathies.   He always had a profound
respect for the man or woman who did useful
work, if the work was done well.   Once, when
a poor woman went to him for advice about some
trifling thing that she had invented, he turned
from his work and explained to her, with the
utmost patience and courtesy, the things that
she wished to know. With his trusted employees,
too, he was usually kindly and sometimes jovial.
"I had only one brush with him in thirty-five
years," said one of his cashiers.   "The last
time that I saw him, he met me on the street
and said, 'Hello, Sellick, have you got lots of
money?   Can you give me a hundred thousand
dollars to-day?'   'Yes, sir,' I answered.   'Well,
I'm glad I don't need it,' he said with a laugh."

The loyalty of his workmen and his agents
was always a source of pride to McCormick.
It was one of the favorite topics of his conversation.   He would mention his men by name and

tell of their exploits with the deepest satisfaction. On one occasion, when a body of agents made a united demand for higher salaries, there was one agent in Minnesota who refused to take part in the movement. "I don't want to force Mr. McCormick," he said. "I have worked for him for nearly thirty years, and I know that he is a just man, and that he will do what is right." Not long afterwards, McCormick was told of this man's action, and he immediately showed his appreciation by making the agent a present of a carriage and fine team of horses.

There was one man who was wholly in Mc-Cormick's power — a negro named Joe, who, by the custom that prevailed in the South before the Civil War, was a slave and the property of McCormick. They were of the same age, and had played together as boys. Joe grew up to be a tall, straight, intelligent negro, and his master was very fond of him. He is mentioned frequently in McCormick's letters, usually in a considerate way. Years before the Civil War McCormick gave Joe his freedom, and some land and a good cabin. Now and then, even in the stress and strain of his business-building, he would stop to write Joe a short letter of good wishes and advice. There was no other one thing, perhaps, which proved so convincingly the essential kindliness of his nature as his treatment of Joe.

In his family relations, too, McCormick was a man of tenderness and devotion. When his father died, in 1846, he was struck down by sorrow. "Many a sore cry have I had as I have gone around this place and found no father," he wrote to his brother William. And as soon as he was solidly established in Chicago, his first act was to send for his mother, and to give her such a royal welcome that she could hardly believe her eyes. "I feel like the Queen of Sheba," she said to her neighbors when she returned to Virginia; "the half was never told."

McCormick helped his younger brothers — William and Leander, by making them his partners. William died in 1865 — a great and irreparable loss. He was a man of careful mind and rare excellence of character, especially able in matters of detail — a point in which Cyrus

McCormick was not proficient. The two men were well suited as partners. Cyrus planned the work in large outlines, and broke down the obstacles that stood in the way; while William added the details and supervised the carrying out of the plan. Leander, who also held a high place in the business in its earlier days, withdrew from it later, and died in 1900.

Until 1858 McCormick had thought himself too busy to be married. But in that year he met Miss Nettie Fowler, of New York, and changed his mind. It was soon apparent that his marriage was not to be in any sense a hindrance to his success, but rather the wisest act of his life. Mrs. McCormick was a woman of rare charm, and with a comprehension of business affairs that was of the greatest possible value to her husband. She was at all times in the closest touch with his purposes. By her advice he introduced many economies at the factory, and rebuilt the works after the Great Fire of 1871. The precision of her memory, and the grasp of her mind upon the multifarious details of human nature and manufacturing, made her

CYRUS HALL McCORMICK. 1883

His Last Portrait

an ideal wife for such a man as Cyrus H. McCormick. As he grew older, he depended upon her judgment more and more; and as Mrs. McCormick is still in the possession of health and strength, it may truly be said that for more than half a century she has been a most influential factor in the industrial and philanthropic development of the United States.

Four sons were born, and two daughters — Cyrus Hall, who is now President of the International Harvester Company; Robert, who died in infancy; Harold, Treasurer of the International Harvester Company; Stanley, Comptroller of the Company; Virginia; and Anita, now known as Mrs. Emmons Blaine.

Mr. McCormick was a most affectionate husband and father. He took the utmost delight in his home and its hospitalities; and invariably brought his whole household with him whenever the growth of his business obliged him to visit foreign countries. In the last few years of his life it gave him the most profound satisfaction to know that his oldest son would pick up the McCormick burden and carry it forward.

"Cyrus is a great comfort to me," he said to an intimate friend. "He has excellent judgment in business matters, and I find myself leaning on him more and more."

The truth is that there was a tender side to McCormick's strong nature, which was not seen by those who met him only upon ordinary occasions. He was in reality a great dynamo of sentiment. He was deeply moved by music, especially by the playing of Ole Bull and the singing of Jenny Lind, who were his favorites. He was as fond of flowers as a child. "I love best the old-fashioned pinks," he said, "because they grew in my mother's garden in Virginia." Often the tears would come to his eyes at the sight of mountains, for they reminded him of his Virginian home. "Oh, Charlie," he said once to his valet, as he sat crippled in a wheel-chair in a Southern hotel, "how I wish I could get on a horse and ride on through those mountains once again!"

McCormick was not in any sense a Gradgrind of commercialism — a man who enriched his coffers by the impoverishment of his soul.

He made money — ten millions or more; but he did so incidentally, just as a man makes muscle by doing hard work. Several of his fellow Chicagoans had swept past him in the million-making race. No matter how much money came to him, he was the same man, with the same friendships and the same purposes. And it is inconceivable that, for any amount of wealth, he would have changed the ground-plan of his life.

It is strictly true to say that he was a practical idealist. He idealized the American Constitution, the Patent Office, the Courts, the Democratic Party, and the Presbyterian Church. He was an Oliver Cromwell of industry. All his beliefs and acts sprang from a few simple principles and fitted together like a picture puzzle. There was religion in his business and business in his religion. He was made such as he was by the Religious Reformation of Europe and the Industrial Revolution of the United States. He was all of one piece — sincere and self-consistent — a type of the nineteenth-century American at his best. He

was not sordid. He was not cynical. He was
not scientific. He was a man of faith and
works — one of the old-fashioned kind who
laid the foundations and built the walls of
this republic.

He felt that he was born into the world with
certain things to do. Some of these things
were profitable and some of them were not, but
he gave as much energy and attention to the
one as to the other. In 1859, for instance, he
had a factory that was profitable, and a daily
paper and a college that were expensive. He
was struggling to extend his trade at home and
in Europe, to protect his patents, to prevent
the war between the North and South, and to
maintain the simplicity of the Presbyterian
faith. To contend for these interests and
principles was his life. He could not have
done anything else. It was as natural for him
to do so as for a fish to swim or a bird to fly.
Once, towards the end of his life, when he was
sitting in his great arm-chair, reflecting, he said
to his wife, "Nettie, life *is* a battle." He made
this announcement as though it were the dis-

covery of a new fact. All his life he had been much less conscious of the battle itself than of the *cause* for which he fought.

In 1884 McCormick died, at that time of the year when wheat is being sown in Spain and reaped in Mexico. The earth-life of "the strong personality before whom obstacles went down as swiftly and inevitably as grain before the knife of his machines," was ended. His last words, spoken in a moment's awakening from the death-stupor, were — "Work, work!" Not even the dissolution of his body could relax the fixity of his will. And when he lay in state, in his Chicago home, there was a Reaper, modelled in white flowers, at his feet; and upon his breast a sheaf of the ripe, yellow wheat, surmounted by a crown of lilies. These were the emblems of the work that had been given him to do, and the evidence of its completion.

CHAPTER XI

THE REAPER AND THE NATION

WHEN Cyrus H. McCormick died in 1884 he had provided hunger-insurance for the United States and the greater part of the civilized world. In that year his own factory made 50,000 harvesting machines, and there were in use, in all countries, more than 500,000 McCormick machines, doing the work of 5,000,000 men in the harvest fields. The United States was producing wheat at the rate of ten bushels per capita, instead of four, as it had been in 1847, when McCormick built his first factory in Chicago. And the total production of wheat in all lands was 2,240,000,000 bushels — enough to give an abundance of food to 325,-000,000 people.

Chicago, in 1884, was a powerful city of six hundred thousand population. It had grown sixty-fold since McCormick rode into it by stage in 1845. It had 3,519 manufacturing establishments, giving work to 80,000 men and women and producing commodities at the rate of $5,000,000 worth in a week. It was then what it is to-day — the chief Reaper City and principal granary of the world. The wheat and flour that were sent out from its ports and depots in the year that the inventor of the Reaper died were enough to make ten thousand million loaves of bread, which, if they were fairly distributed, would have given about forty loaves apiece to the families of the human race.

The United States, in 1884, had been for six years the foremost of the wheat-producing nations. It had also grown to be first in mining, railroads, telegraphs, steel, and agriculture. It was the land of the highest wages and cheapest bread — an anomaly that foreign countries could not understand. In the bulk of its manufacturing, it had forged ahead of all other nations, even of Great Britain; and yet, although a vast army of men had been drawn from its farms to its factories, it had produced in that year more than half a billion bushels of wheat — six times as much as its crop had been in the best year of the sickle and the scythe.

So, in the span of his business life — from 1831 to 1884,— McCormick had seen his country rise from insignificance to greatness, and he had the supreme satisfaction of knowing that his Reaper had done much, if not most, to accelerate this marvellous progress. As we shall see, the invention of the Reaper was the right starting-point for the up-building of a republic. It made all other progress possible, by removing the fear of famine and the drudgery of farm labor. It enabled even the laborer of the harvest-field to be free and intelligent, because it gave him the power of ten men.

The United States as a whole, had paid no attention to the Reaper until the opening of the California gold mines in 1849. Then the sudden scarcity of laborers created a panic among the farmers, and boomed the sale of all manner of farm machinery. Two years later the triumph of the McCormick Reaper at the London Exposition was a topic of the day and a source of national pride. And in 1852 the Crimean War sent the price of wheat skywards,

THE WORKS OF THE McCORMICK HARVESTING MACHINE CO.

providing an English market for as much wheat as American farmers could sell.

But it was not until the outbreak of the Civil War that the United States learned to really appreciate the Reaper. By the time that President Lincoln had made his ninth call for soldiers, by the time that he had taken every third man for the Northern armies, the value of the Reaper was beyond dispute. By a strange coincidence, in this duel between wheat States on the one side, and cotton States on the other, it was a Northerner, Eli Whitney, who had invented the cotton-gin, which made slavery profitable; and it was a Southerner, Cyrus H. McCormick, who had invented the Reaper, which made the Northern States wealthy and powerful.

It was the Reaper-power of the North that offset the slave-power of the South. There were as many Reapers in the wheat-fields of 1861 as could do the work of a million slaves. As the war went on, the crops in the Northern States increased. Europe refused to believe such a miracle; but it was true. Fifty million bushels of American grain went to Europe in 1861, and fifty-six million bushels in the following year. More than two hundred million bushels were exported during the four years of the war. Thus the Reaper not only released men to fight for the preservation of the Union. It not only fed them while they were in the field. It did more. It saved us from bankruptcy as well as famine, and kept our credit good among foreign nations at the most critical period in our history.

After the Civil War came the settling of the West; and here again the Reaper was indispensable. In most cases it went ahead of the railroad. The first Reaper arrived in Chicago three years before the first locomotive. "We had a McCormick Reaper in 1856," said James Wilson; "and at that time there was no railroad within seventy-five miles of our Iowa farm. The Reaper worked a great revolution, enabling one man to do the work that many men had been doing, and do it better. By means of it the West became a thickly settled country, able to feed the nation and to spare bread and meat for the outside world."

When McCormick was a boy, more wheat was raised in Virginia than in any other State. But by 1860 Illinois was ahead, and by degrees the sceptre of the wheat empire passed westwards, until to-day it is held by Minnesota. What with the Homestead Act of 1862, and the offer of McCormick and the other Reaper manufacturers to sell machines to the farmers on credit, it was possible for poor men, without capital, to become each the owner of 160 acres of land, and to harvest its grain without spending a penny in wages. Thus the immense area of the West became a populous country, with cities and railways and State Governments, and producing one-tenth of the wheat of the world.

The enterprise of these Western farmers brought in the present era of farm machinery. It replaced "the man with the hoe" by the man with the self-binder and steel plow and steam thresher. It wiped out the old-time drudge of the soil from American farms, and put in his stead the new farmer, the *business* farmer, who works for a good living and a profit, and not for a bare existence. Such men as Oliver Dalrymple, of North Dakota, led the way by demonstrating what might be done by "bonanza farms." This doughty Scottish-American secured 30,000 acres of the Red River Valley in 1876, and put it all into wheat. It was such a wheat-field as never before had been seen in any country. The soil was turned with 150 gang plows, sown with 70 drills, and reaped with 150 self-binders. Twelve threshing-machines, kept busy in the midst of this sea of yellow grain, beat out the straw and chaff and in the season filled two freight trains a day with enough wheat in each train to give two thousand people their daily bread for a year.

Led on by such pathfinders, American farmers launched out bravely, until now they are using very nearly a billion dollars' worth of labor-saving machinery. The whole level of farm life has been raised. It has been lifted from muscle to mind. The use of machinery has created leisure and capital, and these two have begotten intelligence, education, science, so that the farmer of to-day lives in a new world, and is a wholly different person from what he was when Cyrus McCormick learned to till the soil.

This elevation of the farmer is now seen to be our best guarantee of prosperity and national permanence. It was the incoming flood of wheat money that put the United States on its feet as a manufacturing nation. The total amount of this money, from the building of the first McCormick Reaper factory until to-day, is the unthinkable sum of $5,500,000,000, which may be taken as the net profit of the Reaper to the nation.

Thus the Reaper was not, like the wind-mill, for instance, a mere convenience to the farmer himself. It was the link between the city and the country. It directly benefited all bread-eaters, and put the whole nation upon a higher plane. It built up cities, and made them safe, for the reason that they were not surrounded by hordes of sickle-and-flail serfs, who would sooner or later rise up in the throe of a hunger-revolution and pull down the cities and the palaces into oblivion. When the first Reaper was sold, in 1840, only eight per cent of Americans lived in towns and cities; and to-day the proportion is *forty* per cent. Yet bread is cheaper and more plentiful now than it was then; and there is the most genial and good-natured co-operation between those who live among paved streets and those who live in the midst of the green and yellow wheat-fields. There are no Goths and Vandals on American farms.

Instead of the tiny log workshop on the Mc-Cormick farm, in which the first crude Reaper was laboriously hammered and whittled into shape, there is now a McCormick City in the heart of Chicago — the oldest and largest Harvester plant in the world. In sixty-two years of its life, this plant has produced five or six millions of harvesting machines, and it is still pouring them out at the rate of 7,000 a week. If it were to ship its yearly output at one time, it would require a railway caravan of 14,000 freight-cars to carry the machines from the factory to the farmers.

This McCormick City is one of the industrial wonders that America exhibits to visiting foreigners, and it is so vast that it can only be

McCORMICK REAPER IN USE IN RUSSIA

glanced at in a day.   It covers 229 acres of land.
In its buildings there is enough flooring to cover
a 90-acre farm, and if they were all made over
into one long building, twenty-five feet wide and
one story high, it would be very nearly forty
miles long, as far as from Chicago to Joliet.
The population of McCormick City, counting
workers only, is 7,000, whose average wages
are $2.20 a day.

Here you will find a mammoth twine-mill —
the largest of its kind in any country.   Into this
mill come the bright yellow sisal fibres from
Yucatan and the manila fibres from the Philip-
pines.   These fibres are cleaned and strewn
upon endless chains of combs, which jerk and
pull the fibres and finally deliver them to spindles
— 1,680 spindles, which whirl and twist 19,000
miles of twine in the course of a single day,
almost enough to put a girdle around the
earth.   Most of this work is done by Polish
girls and women, who are being displaced as
farm laborers in their own country by American
harvesting machines.

This plant is so vast that from one point of

view it seems to be mainly a foundry. Thousands of tons of iron — 88,000 tons, to be exact, — pour out of its furnaces every year and are moulded into 113,000,000 castings. But from another point of view it appears to be a carpenter shop. In its yard stand as many piles of lumber as would build a fair-sized city — 60,000,-000 feet of it, cut in the forests of Mississippi and Missouri. And so much of this lumber is being sawed, planed, and shaped in the various wood-working shops that eight sawdust-fed furnaces are needed to supply them with power.

The marvels of labor-saving machinery are upon every hand, in this McCormick City. The paint-tank has replaced the paint-brush. Instead of painting wheels by hand, for instance, ten of them are now strung on a pole, like beads on a string, and soused into a bath from which they come, one minute later, resplendent in suits of red or blue. The labor-cost of painting these ten wheels is two cents. Guard-fingers, for which McCormick paid twenty-four cents apiece in 1845, are now produced with a labor-cost of two cents a dozen. And as for bolts, with two cents you can pay for the making of a hundred. Both bolts and nuts are shaped by automatic machines which are so simple that a boy can operate five at once, and so swift that other boys with wheelbarrows are kept busy carrying away their finished product.

There is one specially designed machine, with a battery of augurs, which bores twenty-one holes at once, thus saving four-fifths of a cent per board. Another special machine shapes poles and saves one cent per pole. Such tiny economies appear absurd, until the immense output is taken into account. Whoever can reduce the costs in the McCormick plant one cent per machine, adds thereby $3,500 a year to the profits, and helps to make it possible for a farmer to buy a magical self-binder, built up of 3,800 parts, for less than the price of a good horse, or for as much wheat as he can grow in one season on a dozen acres.

The vast McCormick City has its human side, too, in spite of all its noise and semi-automatic machinery. Cyrus McCormick was not one of those employers who call their men by numbers

instead of names, and who have no more regard
for flesh and blood than for iron and steel.
He had worked with his hands himself, and
brought up his sons to do the same. The
feeling of loyalty and friendliness between the
McCormick family and their employees has
from the first been unusually strong. In 1902,
at the suggestion of Stanley McCormick, gifts
to the amount of $1,500,000 were made to the
oldest employees of the business, as rewards for
faithful service and tokens of good-will. Also,
a handsome club-house was built for the comfort
of the men of the McCormick City, and a
rest-room for the women, under the mothering
superintendence of a matron and trained nurse.

But this one McCormick City, immense as
it is, does not by any means represent the sum
total of McCormick's legacy to the United
States. As the founder of the harvesting-
machine business, he deserves credit for an industry which now represents an investment of
about $150,000,000. With the sole exception
of the Australian stripper, every wheat-reaping
machine is still made on the lines laid down by

McCormick in 1831. New improvements have been adopted; but not one of his seven factors has been thrown aside.

Fully two-thirds of this industry is still being done by the United States, although four-fifths of the wheat is grown in other countries. Our national income, from this one item of harvesting machinery, has risen to $30,000,000 a year — more than we derive from the exportation of any other American invention. No European country, apparently, has been able to master the complexities and multifarious details which abound in a successful harvester business.

In 1902 the efficiency of the larger American plants was greatly increased by the organization of the International Harvester Company, which has its headquarters in Chicago. The McCormick City is the most extensive plant in this Company, and McCormick's son — who is also Cyrus H. McCormick — is its President. In this Company sixteen separate plants are co-ordinated, four of these being in foreign countries. Its yearly output averages about $75,-000,000 in value; and in bulk is great enough

to fill 65,000 freight-cars. It has 25,000 workmen and 35,000 agents. The lumber with
which its yards are filled comes from its own
80,000-acre forest; the steel comes from its
own furnaces and the iron ore from its own
mines. It is so overwhelmingly vast, this new
famine-fighting consolidation, that the value of
its output for one hour is greater than the
$25,000 of capital with which McCormick built
his first factory in Chicago.

So, it is evident that the McCormick Reaper
has been an indispensable factor in the making
of America. Without it, we could never have
had the America of to-day. It has brought good,
and nothing but good, to every country that has
accepted it. It has never been, and never can
be, put to an evil use. It cannot, under any
system of government, benefit the few and not
the many. It is as democratic in its nature as
the American Constitution; and in every foreign
country where it cuts the grain, it is an educator
as well as a machine, giving to the masses of
less fortunate lands an object-lesson in democracy and the spirit of American progress.

CHAPTER XII

THE REAPER AND THE WORLD

WE shall now see what the invention of the Reaper means to the human race as a whole. We shall leave behind McCormick and the United States, and survey the field from a higher standpoint. The selection of wheat as the first world-food, — its abundance made possible by the Reaper — its transportation by railroads and steamships — its storage in elevators — the production of flour — the growth of wheat-banks, wheat-ports, and exchanges — the new wheat empires — the international mechanism of marketing — the conquest of famine and the stupendous possibilities of the future! These are the subjects that group themselves under the general title — *The Reaper and the World*.

To find a world-food, — that was the beginning of the problem. All human beings wake up hungry every morning of their lives; and consequently the first necessity of the day is food.

The search for food is the oldest of instincts. It is the master-motive of evolution. It has reared empires up and thrown them down. As Buckle has shown, where the national food is cheap and plentiful, population increases more rapidly. And as Sir James Crichton-Browne, in a recent book on "Parcimony in Nutrition," maintains, the lack of food is a prolific cause of war, disease, and social misery in its various forms. "Nothing is more demoralizing," he says, "than chronic hunger."

"For lack of bread the French Revolution failed," said Prince Krapotkin. For lack of bread the opium traffic flourishes in India and China; the secret of the prevalence of opium is that the natives use it to prevent hunger-pangs in time of famine. Once let those countries have cheap bread, and there may be no more opium sold there than there is to-day in Kansas. For lack of bread came the war between Russia and Japan; what the one nation wanted was a seaport for the grain of Siberia, and what the other wanted was more land for the support of her swarming population. For lack of bread

have come most of the crimes of greed and
violence, — most of the social systems based on
sordid self-interest, most of the ill-humor that
has postponed the coming of an era of peace on
earth and good-will among men.

Now, of the three main foods of the human
race, flesh, rice, and wheat, wheat is the best
suited to be a world-food. Flesh becomes too
expensive once the wild game of the forests is
destroyed; and it is not suitable for food in
tropical countries. Rice, on the other hand, is
not a flesh-forming food, and so is not suited
for food in cold countries. Wheat is the one
food that is universal, as good for the Esquimaux
as for the South Sea Islander. It is not easily
spoiled, as milk and fruits are; and it contains
all the elements that are needed by the body and
in just about the right proportion.

Wheat, to the botanist, is a grass — "a de-
graded lily," to quote from Grant Allen. It
was originally a flower that was tamed by man
and trained from beauty to usefulness. We do
not know when or where the prehistoric Bur-
bank lived who undertook this education of the

wheat-lily. But we do know that wheat has
been a food for at least five thousand years.
We find it in the oldest tombs of Egypt and
pictured on the stones of the Pyramids. We
know that Solomon sent wheat as a present
to his friend, the King of Tyre; and we have
reason to believe that its first appearance was
in the valley of the Tigris and the Euphrates,
near where the ancient city of Babylon rose
to greatness.

Wheat is not a wild weed. It is a tame and
transient plant — a plant of civilization. It
could not continue to exist without man, and
man, perhaps, could not exist except in the
tropical countries without wheat. Each needs
the other. If the human race were to perish
from the face of the earth, wheat might survive
for three years, but no longer. So close has
this co-operation been between wheat and civilized man, that an eminent German writer, Dr.
Gerland, maintains with a wealth of evidence
that wheat was the original cause of civilization,
partly because it was the first good and plentiful
food, and partly because it was wheat that

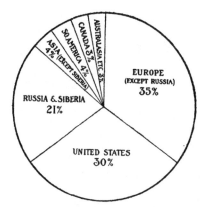

Chart Showing Relative Distribution of Values by
Producing Countries in 1908 of World's Production of Five Principal Grains. Approximate Value, $9,280,000,000

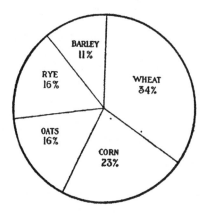

Chart Showing Relative Values in 1908 of World's
Production of the Five Principal Grains.
Approximate Value, $9,280,000,000

persuaded primitive man to forsake his wars and
his wanderings and to learn the peaceful habits
of agriculture.

In any case, whatever its earlier history may
have been, wheat is to-day the chief food of the
civilized races of mankind. It is the main
support of 600,000,000 people. It has overcome its natural enemies — weeds, fungus
diseases, insects, and drought, — and attained
a crop total of 3,500,000,000 bushels a year.
To the intelligent, purposeful nations that have
become the masters of the human race, wheat
is now the staff of life, the milk of Mother Earth,
the essence of soil and air and rain and sunshine.

But, although wheat was known to be the
best food for fifty centuries, it did not until very
recently, until thirty or forty years ago, become
a world-food. Every community ate up its own
wheat. It had little or none to sell, because, no
matter how much grain the farmers planted,
they could not in the eight or ten days of harvest
gather more than a certain limited quantity into
their barns. All that one man could do, with
his wife to help him, was to snatch in enough

wheat to feed ten people for a year. Each family could do no more than feed one other family and itself. This was the Tragedy of the Wheat. There was never enough of it. It was so precious that none could be sure of it except the kings and the nobilities. As for the masses of peasantry who sowed the wheat and reaped it with hand-sickles, they would almost as soon have thought of wearing diamonds as of eating white bread.

Then, in 1831, came the Reaper. It was not invented in any of the older countries, nor in any of the great cities of the world. For five thousand years neither the peasants nor the kings had conceived of any better way of reaping wheat than with the sickle and the scythe. The man who had cut the Gordian knot of Famine was the son of a citizen-farmer, Cyrus Hall McCormick by name, Scotch-Irish by race, American by birth, and inventor by heredity and early training.

This new machine, the Reaper, when it was full-grown into the self-binder, was equal to forty sickles. With one man to drive it, it could cut and bind enough wheat in one season to feed four hundred people. In its most highly developed form, the combined harvester and thresher, it has become so gigantic a machine that thirty-two horses are required to haul it. This leviathan cuts a fifty-foot roadway through the grain, threshes it and bags it at the rate of one bag every half-minute. And the total world production of Reapers of every sort — self-binders, mowers, headers, corn-binders, etc.,— is probably as many as 1,500,000 a year, two-thirds of them being made in the United States.

Because of this harvesting machinery, the wheat crop of the world is now nearly twice what it was in 1879. The American crop has multiplied six and a half times in fifty years. Western Canada, Australia, Siberia, and Argentina have become wheat producers. The cost of growing one bushel in America, with machinery and high wages, is now about half a dollar, which is less than the cost in Europe and as low as the cost in India, where laborers can be hired for a few pennies a day. With a sickle, the time-cost of a bushel of wheat was three

hours; with a self-binder, it is now ten minutes.
And so, because of these amazing results, the
rattle of the harvester has become an indispensable part of the music of our industrial orches-
tra, harmonious with the click of the telegraph
key, the ring of the telephone bell, the hum of
the sewing-machine, the roar of the Bessemer
converter, the gong of the trolley, the whistle
of the steamboat, and the puff of the locomotive.

Next to the Reaper, the most important factors in this world-mechanism of the bread, are
the Railroad and the Steamboat. These arrived on the scene just at the right time to dis-
tribute the surplus that the Reaper produced.
The Steamboat, and its humble relative, the
barge, came first. The Erie Canal of 1825,
the Suez Canal of 1869, and the Sault Ste.
Marie Canal of 1881, were built largely for
the carrying of the wheat. By 1856 wheat was
on its way from Chicago to Europe; and four
years later the first wheat-ship curved around
Cape Horn from California. Ten years ago
an entirely new kind of ship, a sort of immense
steel bag called a "whaleback," was built to

carry 250,000 bushels of wheat in a single load. By this means a ton of wheat is actually carried thirteen miles for one cent.   There are to-day small barges on the canals of Holland, large ones on the river Volga, and several thousand steamships on the world's main water-ways, all carrying burdens of wheat.   Enough is now being transported from port to port to give steady work to fully three hundred steamships and summer work to very nearly as many more.

There was an exciting contest between the ship and the car in the earlier days of transportation, to see which should carry the largest share of the wheat.   About 1869 the car won. In this year, too, the United States was belted with a railway, east to west, which meant the opening up of the first great wheat-empire. Other railways pushed out into the vast prairies of the West, lured by the call of the wheat. They were the pioneers of the world's wheat-railways.   Wheat was their chief freight and wheat farmers were their chief passengers.   At the outset the grain was shipped in bags.   Then some railway genius invented the grain-car, which holds as much as twenty or twenty-five wagons. And to-day one of the ordinary moving pictures of an American railroad is a sixty-car train travelling eastward with enough wheat in its rolling bins to give bread to a city of ten thousand people for a year.

The trans-Siberian railway, which is the longest straight line of steel in the world, was built largely as a wheat-conveyor. So were the railways of western Canada, Argentina, and India. Ever since the advent of the Reaper wheat has been the prolific mother of railways and steamships. While the rice nations are still putting their burdens on ox-carts and on the backs of camels and elephants, the wheat nations have built up a system of transportation that is a daily miracle of cheapness, efficiency, and speed. This system is not yet finished. A new line of steamships is about to be set afloat between Buenos Ayres and Hamburg. The Erie Canal is being re-made, at a fabulous cost, so that a steamer with 100,000 bushels of wheat can go directly from Buffalo to New York. And an adventurous railway is now pushing its

way north from the wheat-fields of western
Canada to the unknown water of Hudson Bay,
whence the wheat will be carried by boat to
London and Liverpool.

To-day it is not the long haul of wheat, but
the short haul, that is more expensive. It is
cheaper to carry wheat from one country to
another than from the barn to the nearest town.
The average distance that an American farmer
has to haul his grain is nine and a half miles,
and the average cost of haulage is nine cents per
hundred pounds. Thus it has actually become
true that to carry wheat ten miles by wagon
costs more than 2,300 miles by steamship.
Such is the tense efficiency of our wheat-carrier
system that a bushel of grain can now be picked
up in Missouri and sent to the cotton-spinners
of England for a dime.

Associated with this transportation problem
was the matter of storage. There was no sort
of a building known to man, fifty years ago, in
which a million bushels of wheat might be con-
veniently kept. An entirely new kind of building had to be invented. All the wheat barns

were overflowing. All the warehouses were
outgrown. The difficulty was to make a huge
building that could be quickly filled and emptied.
Then, at the precise moment when he was
needed, an inventor, F. H. Peavey, appeared
with a device for elevating grain — an endless
carrier to which metal cups were fastened.
From this idea the *elevator* was born.

The first city that appreciated the usefulness
of this new, unlovely building was Chicago. It
became not only the home of the Reaper, but
also the main storehouse of the wheat. It
erected one after another of these mastodonic
buildings until to-day thirty-six of them stand
along the water-front, roomy enough to hold
the entire crop of Holland, Sweden, Greece,
Egypt, Mexico, and New Zealand. What these
immense grain-bins have done for the prosperity
of Chicago would require many books to tell
completely. It was largely because of them
that Chicago outgrew Berlin and became the
central metropolis of North America, with
twenty-six railways emptying their freight at

MAMMOTH WHEAT-FIELD IN SOUTH DAKOTA WITH TWENTY HARVESTERS IN LINE

her doors and seven thousand vessels a year arriving at her harbor.

At present Chicago has swung from wheat to corn and oats, and enabled Minneapolis to become the greatest actual wheat-storage city of the world.   In Minneapolis the owning of elevators has become a profession.   There are not only forty-four elevators in the city itself, but also forty elevator companies that have built more than two thousand elevators in the wheat States of the Northwest.   The Jumbo of all elevators is here — a stupendous granary that holds 6,000,000 bushels, as much as may be reaped by two thousand self-binders from seven hundred square miles of land.

Of all American cities, there are only five others that can put roofs over 10,000,000 bushels of grain.   Duluth-Superior stands at the head of these, with twice the storage capacity of New York.   This double city, with the picturesque location, Duluth on her Minnesota hillside and Superior on her Wisconsin plain, has in recent years overtaken all competitors and is now the leading wheat-shipping port in the world. Buffalo comes next as an elevator city, having twenty-eight towering buildings of steel operated by the energy of Niagara Falls. Even this famous cataract helps a little in the making of cheap bread. New York follows closely after Buffalo; with Kansas City and St. Louis running neck and neck at quite a distance behind. It is an odd fact that there is not one elevator on the Pacific coast. Because of the rainless weather, the wheat is put into bags and piled outdoors until the day of shipment. This is an expensive method of handling, as the bags cost four cents apiece and no machine has as yet been invented that will pick up and handle a sack of grain.

The American elevator has now been very generally adopted as the ideal wheat-bin. Two Roumanian cities, Braila and Galatz, have suggested an improvement by using concrete instead of steel. And one Russian city, Novorossisk, on the Black Sea, has introduced a most original feature in the building of elevators by erecting a very large one a quarter of a mile back from the dock, because of the better view that this site affords of the harbor.

London has no elevators, and never has had, although it buys more wheat than any other city. It has six million mouths to feed, so that the grain is devoured as fast as it arrives. To give bread to London would take the entire crop of Indiana or Siberia. Neither are there any elevators of any importance in Paris, Berlin, or Antwerp. Whatever wheat arrives at these cities is either hurried to the mill or re-shipped. Wheat is too precious in Europe to be stored for a year or for two years, as may happen in Minnesota. Rotterdam has one elevator only and of moderate size. Neither Odessa nor Sulina have any of the large pro-portions, for the reasons that in Odessa the labor unions have an unconquerable prejudice against elevators, and in Sulina the grain is held only a short time and then forwarded else-where. This Sulina, as a glance at the map of Europe will show, is the loneliest of all the wheat-cities. It stands on a heap of gravel at the mouth of the Danube — an oasis of human

life in a vast marshy wilderness. The children
born there have never seen a railway; but 1,400
ships leave the stone docks of Sulina every year
laden with enough wheat to feed London, Paris,
and Berlin. To find the exact reverse of Sulina, we must go to Buenos Ayres — the premier
wheat-city of South America and the gayest of
them all. Built up at first by the cattle trade,
and now depending mainly upon wheat, this
superb city has become the topmost pinnacle
of South American luxury and refinement. It
has several new elevators, erected by the railway companies.

After the Reaper, the Railway, the Steamship, and the Elevator, came the Exchange.
This, too, came first in Chicago, in its modern
form. There was one little grain Exchange in
the Italian city of Genoa, several centuries ago,
and England points back to 1747 as the year
when her first Corn Exchange was born. But
it was the Exchange in Chicago, started by
thirteen men in 1848, that first came into
its full growth and became an arena of international forces.

A wheat Exchange is to-day much more than a meeting-place for brokers. It is a mechanism. It is a news bureau — a parliament — a part of the whispering-gallery of the world. It not only provides a market where wheat can at once be bought and sold, but it obtains for both buyer and seller all the news from everywhere about the wheat, so that no bargain may be made in the dark. Before Exchanges were organized there were times when a farmer would drive twenty miles to the nearest town with a load of wheat, and find no one to buy it. Even in Chicago, in the early forties, a farmer ran the risk of not being able to trade his wheat for a few groceries.

At present, when a buyer or a seller of wheat arrives at an Exchange, he goes at once to consult the weather map of the day. From here he passes to a series of bulletin-boards, which inform him of the arrival or outgo of wheat at many cities. One board tells him the visible supply of wheat in the world, so that he can easily ascertain, if he wishes to do so, *how much bread the human race ate last week.* Other boards have telegrams and cablegrams of disaster — frost in Alberta, hail in Minnesota, green bug in Texas, rust in Argentina, drought in Australia, locusts in Siberia, monsoon in India, and chinch bug in Missouri. Good news is here, too, as well as bad. There may be reports of a record-breaking crop in Roumania, an opulent rain in Kansas, a new steamship line from Kurrachee to Liverpool, and the plowing of a million acres of new land in western Canada. And also there are, of course, the records of the latest sales and prices in other Exchanges.

Thus the farmer can not only find a ready buyer for his wheat. He can, by means of a newspaper or a telephone, know what price he ought to receive, as all the news gathered by the Exchanges is freely given to the public. Such is the perfection of the news mechanism that has been built up around the marketing of the wheat, that before a Dakota farmer starts out for town with a load of grain, he can go to the telephone under his own roof and learn the prices at various cities and the world-conditions of the wheat trade.

The paper which best deserves to be called the official journal of the wheat is the *Corn Trade News*, of Liverpool; and the building which best deserves to be called the international headquarters of the wheat business is the handsome new Baltic Exchange, near by the Bank of England in London. This Baltic market is so practically international, in fact, that it is never closed. Whoever wishes to buy or sell wheat may do so here at any hour of the day or night. There are no days in this building and no seasons, for the reason that it is always noonday and harvest-time in some part of the world. In this Baltic Exchange, too, there is now a nucleus for a Wheat Parliament, organized under the name of the Corn Trade Association. This society has undertaken to put the wheat business in order, by establishing standard contracts, collecting samples of all wheats, arbitrating disputes, and condemning all dishonesties of whatever sort.

As wheat Exchange cities, London, Liverpool, and Chicago outclass all others. Neither Italy nor France have any central or dominating market. In Paris, Antwerp, Hamburg, and Amsterdam the Bourses, as the Exchanges are called, are public buildings, and the members of each Bourse represent the local situation and nothing more. One of the most ambitious and speculative of the European Exchanges is the one at Budapest, which stands beside a dainty little park where the brokers eat their lunch in fine weather; and the youngest of all Exchanges is the one that was born in Buenos Ayres in 1908, representing a surplus of a hundred million bushels a year.

Besides the brokers, in their Exchanges, there must also be inspectors in the marketing of the wheat. In some countries these inspectors are government officers, as in Germany and Canada; and elsewhere they are local officials or private employees, as in the United States. A carload of wheat, passing from Dakota to New York, will probably have from three to six inspections.

Also, the insurance agent takes his place in the

HARVESTING IN ROUMANIA

circle of co-operation when the wheat begins to move from barn to bakery. He insures the wheat in the elevators, on the cars, or in the steamships. He may even insure it against hail and tornadoes while it is growing. It is so precious, this brown seed, that we watch over every step of its progress.

It is the bankers' busy season, too, when the wheat begins to move. The marketing of the grain ties up more money than any other yearly event. "It threatens us with disaster every fall," said one of the Secretaries of the Treasury, when making a plea for a more elastic currency. "We ship half a million dollars a day during harvest," said the president of a Chicago bank. "We drew more than five millions of currency from the East and sent thirty-eight millions to the country during September and October of last year," said a third financier, who spoke for Chicago as a whole. In short, the movement of the wheat means a matter of five hundred millions to American bankers; and it is the most important occurrence of the year to the bankers of Russia, Canada, Argentina, and Australia.

Many a bank, as well as many a railroad, was founded upon the moving of the wheat.

The broker, the banker, the inspector, and the insurance agent — these four render a useful service to the wheat that has left home; but there is a fifth man about whose usefulness there is the widest possible difference of opinion — the speculator. From one point of view, the speculator is the driving-wheel of the whole wheat trade. By his energy and his impetus he steadies and equalizes the conflicting forces, and gives the entire mechanism a continuous movement. From another point of view, he is a gambler, reckless and parasitical, who interferes with the natural laws of supply and demand, and snatches an unearned toll from the wheat bins of the world.

Some of the wheat nations not only permit speculation in wheat, but practically encourage it by allowing more privileges to the speculator than to the ordinary business man. Others are resolutely stamping it out, as a nuisance and a crime. The nations that have voted "Yea" on speculation are Great Britain, Hungary, Sweden,

Norway, France, and the United States; and the nations that have voted "Nay" are Germany, Holland, Belgium, Australia, Switzerland, Greece, and Argentina. Canada has been divided on the question, since the Province of Manitoba broke up the Winnipeg Grain Exchange by legislation in 1908.

In the end, as organization increases, speculation will decline. Chicago will try to push prices up and London will try to pull them down; but there will be fewer violent fluctuations. Better methods of farming and a more reliable system of news-gathering will eliminate the element of chance to such an extent that the wheat trade will offer less and less scope for speculation and no inducements at all to the reckless plunger. Already the frantic methods of marketing wheat have been outgrown in the Exchanges of Liverpool and London. In neither of these places is there any Wheat Pit, or any maelstrom of frenzied brokers. Without any shouting or jostling or wild tumult of any kind, the English brokers are buying two hundred million bushels of wheat a year, and controlling the situation to a greater extent than any other body of men. This, too, without any restrictive legislation.

Before wheat was made plentiful by the Reaper, it was possible for a daring man to establish a corner or monopoly; but no one has succeeded in doing this for more than forty years. The last wheat corner that did not fail was in 1867. Since then every would-be cornerer has been caught in his own trap. The wheat-machinery of the world has now become so vast that no individual can master it. Whoever has tried it has found that he was being cornered by the wheat; for as soon as he had raised the price to an artificial level, the grain has flowed in upon him and covered him up. The price of wheat to-day may be temporarily deflected by schemes and conspiracies, but not for long. Ultimately it is decided by the state of the crop and the state of public opinion in the thirty-six countries that grow wheat and eat bread.

Within the last thirty years, since the Reaper has come into universal use, the area of the world's wheat-field has doubled. New coun-

tries have arisen, that were only waste places
before. The habitable earth has grown im-
mensely larger. There is more room for both
wheat and men to grow, and less scope for the
forestaller and the monopolist. Just as the
Reaper was the advance-machine of civilization across the prairies of the West, so it is
to-day opening up new territories and developing new resources.

Northwestern Canada, for instance, was a
dozen years ago supposed to be a barren wilderness of snow and ice, in which none but the
hunter and the fur-trader might earn a living.
Then several adventurous Minnesotans went
across and planted wheat. It grew — forty
bushels to the acre, and the acres, there were
two hundred million of them, were waiting for
the plow and almost to be had for the asking.
Since then, more than three hundred thousand
American farmers have swept across the line
and joined in the greatest wheat-rush of this
generation. Twelve hundred grain elevators
have been built along the line of the Canadian
Pacific; and Chicago self-binders rattled through

the yellow wheat last Summer two thousand miles north of St. Louis.

In Argentina, too, and Australia, where the wheat ripens just in time to decorate the Christmas trees, there is to be seen the same conquest of nature. Desolate plains are being tamed by the plow and exploited by the harvesters. In the semi-arid belt that lies east of the Rocky Mountains, new kinds of wheat, less thirsty, are being taught to grow. In Russia and Siberia a vast tract of twenty-five million acres has been rescued from idleness in the last fifteen years. And even in the valley of the Euphrates, where wheat, so it is believed, was born, a new railway is now being constructed which, when it is finished, will carry oil and wheat.

By thus opening up new regions to settlement, the wheat-farmer not only thwarts the monopolist and makes the world a larger place to live in, he does more: he compels the gold to come out of its vaults in the great cities and to flow to the outermost parts of the earth. For every eighteen thousand pounds of wheat that go to the city, there will go back to the farmer one

pound of gold.   For every loaf of bread upon a
Londoner's table, there will go a cent and a half
to the man behind the Reaper.   And so, the
sale of every wheat-crop means that the gold
will come throbbing out into the arteries of
business, like the blood from the heart, and on
its way back and forth nourish the whole body
of the nation.

It is in the very nature of the wheat trade to
benefit the masses and not the few.   The more
wheat that grows, the less danger there is of an
aristocracy of wheat.   More wheat means more
luxury in the farmhouse, more traffic on the
railway, and more food in the slums.   It
means busier factories and steel-mills, because
the farmer, when he receives his wheat-money,
becomes the customer of the manufacturer.
Thus it was not at all accidental that the wealth
of Buenos Ayres came with the exportation of
wheat, or that the commercial awakening of
Canada followed the opening up of her western
prairies, or that the industrial supremacy of the
United States dates from the immense wheat
harvests that began in 1880 to push the whole

country forward with the power of $500,000-000 a year. As one of McCormick's competitors, J. D. Easter of Evanston, once declared, "It seems as though the McCormick Reaper started the ball of prosperity rolling, and it has been rolling ever since."

If we wish to know what the Reaper will eventually do for these new wheat countries, we have but to glance back over the short history of our ten prairie States. Here, by the use of both science and machinery, the New Farmer has reached his highest level of success. By 1884 these ten States had twenty million thriving settlers, riding on forty-two thousand miles of railway, raising as much wheat in a day as New England could in a year, and storing their profits in twenty-five hundred banks. Incredible as it may seem to Europe and Asia, it is true that even the poorhouses in Iowa and Kansas were used last year as storehouses for wheat. And it is true that in the co-operative commonwealth called Kansas, at the last assessment, there were found to be forty-four thousand pianos and six million dollars' worth

HARVESTING HEAVY GRAIN, SOUTH AMERICA

of carriages and automobiles. This in a State where there are no Grand Dukes and where every man works for a living!

If the lords of Siberia wish to know what may be done with that famine-swept vastitude they may come and see that bed of an ancient sea, which in thirty years has been transformed into the world's greatest bread-land — the Red River Valley. Here the banks are not only packed with millions, but hundreds of millions, belonging to the shirt-sleeved proprietors of the soil. Here, in the yellow days of August, a man may travel for days and see no limit to the ocean of waving, shimmering wheat, that ripples around him in a vast sky-bounded circle. Wheat — wheat — wheat! Nothing but wheat! It is a Field of the Cloth of Gold, that adds nothing to the glory of kings, but much to the glory of the common people. Drop the German Empire down upon this valley and its expanse of dizzying, swirling wheat, and the wheat would not be wholly eclipsed. There would still be enough grain around the edges to make a golden fringe.

The children born and bred in this Red River Valley have never seen, except in pictures, a sickle or a flail. Their only conception of a harvest time is that a battery of red self-binders, with reels whirling and knives clacking, shall charge upon the wheat as though each acre were a battalion of hostile infantry, and make war until the land is strewn with heaps of fallen sheaves. Famine, to these children of the wheat, seems as remote a danger as the cooling of the sun. Even the one young State of North Dakota, not yet of age, is now growing food for herself, and for twelve million people besides.

So, the urgent world-problem is to teach other nations the lesson of the Red River Valley. There is not yet enough bread so that we may put a loaf at every plate. To feed the whole race according to the present American standard of living would require ten thousand million bushels — three times as much as we are raising now; and the demand is fast outgrowing the supply. Sooner or later the Chinese will learn to eat at least one loaf a week apiece, and when they do, it will mean that the world's wheat crop must be increased ten per cent.

More wheat and a more efficient organization of wheat agencies — that is the programme of the future.   Already one unsuccessful effort has been made to hold an international Wheat Congress;   and the second attempt may end more happily.   Now that the world has become so small that a cablegram flashes completely around it in twelve minutes;   now that there are forty-four nations united by The Hague Conferences and fifty-eight by the Postal Union;   now that war has grown to be so expensive that one cannon-shot costs as much as a college education and one battleship as much as a first-class University,— it is quite probable that the march of co-operation will continue until there is a Congress, and a central headquarters and a Tribunal, which will represent nothing less than an international fellowship of the wheat.

CHAPTER XIII

GIVE US THIS DAY OUR DAILY BREAD

WE have now seen the machinery by which the wheat is cut, moved, stored, financed, and marketed. Its next and last step, as wheat, is to the Flour-mill, whence it goes to the bakeries, the groceries, and the homes of six hundred million people. Here, too, there have had to come new methods since the advent of the Reaper.

In the Dark Ages of the sickle and the flail, two flat stones did well enough for a flour-mill. Even the bread that was found in the ruins of Pompeii had been made of wheat that was merely crushed. Later came the mill run by horse-power or by the energy of a little stream. Such were the first American mills. The mill that was operated by George Washington at Mount Vernon, for instance, was run by water-power and produced flour that sold for thirteen dollars a barrel. Rochester, N. Y., was the first American "Flour City"; but the modern flour-mill did not come until it was compelled to come by the deluge of Reaper wheat that flooded the markets in 1870.

As usually happens in the case of inventions, it came where it was not expected. It made its arrival in the Hungarian city of Budapest in 1874. The "new process," as it was called, was based upon the use of steel rolls instead of stones. It was as superior to the old-fashioned way as the Reaper had been to the sickle or as the thresher was to the flail. It was amazingly quick and produced a better flour. By reason of these new mills, Budapest became at a bound the foremost "Flour City" of the world, and held its place against all comers until 1890.

Then the prestige passed to Minneapolis — a young city on the head-waters of the Mississippi, the recent home of the prairie-dog and the buffalo. Shortly before the Civil War, a youthful lawyer named William D. Washburn drifted westwards from Maine until he came to Minneapolis, at that time a tiny village on the frontier. He found no clients here, and no law; but he did find a ledge of limestone rock jutting across the Mississippi and making the only large water-fall in all that region. So he threw aside his legal education and became the organizer of a water-power company and the owner of a little flour-mill. Soon the long line of Reapers reached Minneapolis and swept on westwards into the richest wheat lands that had ever been known. The wheat overwhelmed the slow old-fashioned mills, so the ex-lawyer in 1878 adopted the Budapest system and built a roller-mill that was the quickest and most automatic of its kind. Other millers had by this time come to Minneapolis — Pillsbury, Crosby, Christian, and Dunwoody; and all together they pushed the flour business until in twelve years they had become the main millers of the world.

To-day the river of wheat is deepest at Minneapolis. Its twenty-two great mills roll 120,-000,000 bushels into flour as an ordinary year's work. While the swiftest mill in Athens, in the age of Pericles, produced no more than two barrels a day, there is one mill of incredible size in Minneapolis that fills *seventeen thousand* barrels in a twenty-four hours' run — enough

INDIANS REAPING THEIR HARVEST, WHITE EARTH, MINNESOTA

to give bread to New York State and California. What the Greeks did in a day the Minnesotans do in ten seconds. Five million barrels of this Minneapolis flour is each year scattered among foreign nations, a fact which informs us that flour is now not a local product, but part of the real currency of nations. No doubt the people who dwell by the Sea of Galilee, whose fathers were once miraculously fed upon seven loaves of bread and a few fishes, are now being fed miraculously upon loaves of bread made from the flour of Minneapolis.

The making of the bread — that is the final step in this movement of the wheat. As yet, this is a local process, though not wholly so. Certain ready-to-eat foods are now being made from wheat and boxed in such a way that they may be sent from one country to another. If we trace back the original of a loaf of bread of ordinary size, we shall find that it was made from two-thirds of a pound of flour, which was rolled from one pound of wheat, containing about twelve thousand grains that were grown on forty-eight square feet of land and reaped

by a self-binder in two seconds. When the
wheat was cut in the old-fashioned way, with a
hand-sickle, every loaf of bread required eighty
seconds' labor instead of two.

In a public test made last year in the State
of Washington, wheat was cut, threshed, ground
into flour, and baked into biscuits in twenty-
three minutes. This is an evidence that all the
machinery for handling grain has now been
brought up to the same high level of speed and
efficiency as the self-binder. It also helps us to
understand the daily marvel of cheap bread —
the fact that a hundred loaves of bread are now
delivered one by one at an American workingman's door for the cost of a seat at the opera or
a couple of song-records by Caruso.

So plentiful is this bread that the loaves baked
from American flour in 1907 would have made
a wall of bread around the earth, or have given
thirty loaves apiece to every human creature;
and so cheap has it become in these latter days
that even in the United States it is not more
than three cents a day per capita. The unskilled laborer who receives $1.50 a day, earns

his bread in the first ten minutes, every work day morning. And the total tax he pays to the men who make the self-binders is not more than one tenth of a cent per loaf.

Three-sevenths of the people of the world are now on a wheat basis. They are the lesser fraction in point of numbers, but the larger in point of prosperity and progress. A wheat map of the globe would be very nearly a map of modern civilization. As yet, there are many peasants who grow wheat and cannot afford to eat it. But the number of bread-eaters is steadily increasing, probably at the rate of four or five million a year.

The nation that eats most bread per capita is Belgium. After her come France, England, and the United States. As the Belgians, with their scanty acres, cannot grow more wheat than would support them for nine weeks, they are compelled to import nearly fifty million bushels a year; and it is this continual influx of grain that has done most to make Antwerp the third busiest port in the world and the home of forty steamship lines.

France is second as an eater, and third as a grower, of wheat. But it is not an important factor in the international market, as there is usually almost an even balance between what it grows and what it eats. It has very little either to buy or to sell. Its crops are steady and large, and by intensive cultivation the thrifty French are obtaining the same amount of grain from less and less land.

There are two countries only, Great Britain and Holland, that impose no tariff upon either wheat or flour. Neither the British nor the Dutch will tolerate a bread tax. Both countries have barely enough land to grow one-quarter as much wheat as they need, although there was a period in the early history of England when it was nicknamed "the Granary of the North," because of its many wheat-fields. To-day the bread on three British tables out of four is made of wheat brought in a British ship from some foreign country; and the total amount of wheat consumed in the United Kingdom is so great that it requires an army of 93,000 men with self-binders to cut it and tie it into sheaves.

If it had to be reaped with sickles, it would be a ten-day harvesting for half the able-bodied men in the two islands.

Germany eats less wheat than Great Britain, and raises more than twice as much. The Germans are skilled wheat-farmers. They grow as much on half an acre of poor soil as Americans grow on a whole acre of good soil. The Italians eat very nearly as much as the Germans, and raise a larger crop by dint of great labor on the tiny farms and terraced hillsides of Italy. Both countries tax the bread of the poor by a tariff of thirty-eight to forty-eight cents a bushel on foreign wheat. The Austrians and Hungarians, in spite of a climate of extremes and sudden changes, manage to supply themselves with more than ten billion loaves of bread by the tillage of their own fields, and usually have some flour to sell to the neighboring countries. The Spanish cannot quite feed themselves; in addition to the wheat they grow, they are obliged to buy about a hundred ship-loads a year. Denmark comes out even. Portugal buys her bread for four months of the year. Greece, Norway, and Sweden raise half enough wheat. The Swiss can get no more from their valley-farms than will feed them for ten weeks. And the peasants of Russia and Roumania, who raise wheat in abundance, have unfortunately not yet risen to that luxurious level of life in which white bread is the every-day food of the people. Although Russia has more wheat to sell than any other nation, a Russian eats one-third as much wheat as a Belgian, and there is a famine somewhere in the vast Russian Empire almost every winter.

Africa is not yet a wheat-eating continent. Egypt, which was, in the Golden Age of the Pharaohs, the wheat-centre of the world, now grows less grain than Oregon; Algeria raises less than Ohio; and Tunis, from the fields that surround the ruins of ancient Carthage, produces less grain than Tennessee. India is slowly shifting from rice to wheat. Many of the fields that once grew indigo are now yellow with grain. At present India is the most uncertain factor in the situation, as it may have eighty million bushels to sell or none. As it is one-third as large as the United States, and crowded

A HARVEST SCENE UPON A RUSSIAN ESTATE.

with three times the population, there is always
need of its grain at home. As yet, the Reaper
has not been allowed to extend its benefits to
India. Most of the grain is reaped in the old
slow, wasteful way. It is sown by hand, cut by
sickles, stored in pits, and transported on the
backs of camels. Little Japan is falling into
line as a bread-eating country, growing now as
much wheat as California. And even China,
which is not as a whole on the wheat-map
of the world, has recently begun to grow
wheat in Manchuria and to build flour-mills
at Hong-Kong.

So, the human race will soon be able to feed
itself. It has learned how and needs only to use
to the full the agencies that are already invented
and established. Beginning with the McCormick Reaper in 1831, there has been constructed
a world mechanism of the bread, which promises to wholly abolish Famine and its brood of
evils. The crude machine that was hammered
and whittled into shape in a log workshop on a
Virginian farm, has now become a System — a
McCormick System, that cuts ten million bushels

of ripe wheat a day and transports it hither and thither as handily as though the whole round earth were girt with belt-conveyors.

That young Virginian farmer who awoke from his dream and made his dream come true, made it possible for a few in each country to provide enough food for all. He found a cure for Hunger, which had always persisted like a chronic disease. He heaped the plates on the tables of thirty-six nations. He took a drudgery and transformed it into a profession. He instructed the wheat-eating races how to increase the "seven small loaves" so that the multitudes should be fed. He picked up the task of feeding the hungry masses — the Christly task that had lain unfulfilled for eighteen centuries, and led the way in organizing it into a system of international reciprocity.

To-day there is no longer in most countries any tragic note in the Epic of the Wheat. There is no sweating peasant with a hoe. The plowman may even sit, it he wishes, upon the sliding steel knife that slices the soil into furrows, or upon the steel harrow that combs the clods into

soft, loose earth. The sower is no heavy-footed
serf, scattering his grain in handfuls upon the
surface of the soil, where the birds of the air may
devour it. He, too, rides upon a machine with
steel fingers that plant the living seed securely
in the living earth. And when, at the call of the
sun and the rain, the black field becomes green
and ripens from green to gold, its yellow fruitage
is swept down and into barns, not by a horde of
stooping laborers, but by the Grand March of
the Harvesters, the drivers of painted chariots,
who ride against the grain and leave it behind
them in bound sheaves.

Henceforth civilization may be based upon
higher motives than the Search for Food. The
struggle for existence may become the struggle
of the nobler nature for its full development.
The gentle need not be eliminated by the strong.
Instead of contending with one another in an
unbrotherly competition, men may move up-
ward to the higher activities of social self-preservation and organized self-help. By mastering
the problem of the bread, they have opened up
such opportunities for education, for travel, for

happier homes, for the prosperity and friendship
of the nations, as no previous generation has
ever had.   And it is here, it is in this larger and
kindlier civilization, that is now made possible
by the Reaper and the wheat-mechanism which
has grown up around it, that we shall find the
full spiritual value to the world of that stout-
hearted bread-winner of the human race whose
life began among the hills of Old Virginia one
hundred years ago.

THE END

INDEX

INDEX

A

Adams, John, 15

Adriance, John P., 103, 119

Advertisements of Reaper, 54, 81–83, 112, 134

Africa not a wheat-eating country, 242

Agencies established for sale of Reapers (about 1844), 63

Agents, Cyrus H. McCormick's plan in regard to, 83, 84, 86

Agriculture, Department of, 87

Albert, Prince, 125, 132

Algeria, 242

Allen, Grant, 205

America, yacht, 131

Amsterdam, 222

Antwerp, no grain stored in, 217; Bourse in, 222; third busiest port in world, 239

Appleby, John F., 115

Argentina, 209, 212, 225, 228

Arkwright, inventor, 53, 131

Armagh massacre of 1641, 22

Athens, mills at, 236

Atkins, Jearum, 106

Augusta County, Virginia, 3

Australia, wheat crop of, 209; legislation against speculation in, 225; development of, 228

Australian stripper, 200

Austria in 1809, 4; farm laborers received no wages in, 123; climate and wheat production in, 241

Austrian Emperor decorated Cyrus H. McCormick, 135

Ayrshire, Scotland, 86

B

Babylon, 206

Baggage Case, 1862–1885, 100 –102; *see also* Pennsylvania Railroad

Baltic Exchange, London, 221

Baltic, holder of ocean record, 131

Baltimore and Ohio Railway, 49

Baltimore Convention of 1861, 158, 166

Bankers concerned in moving of wheat, 223, 224

Barbary pirates, 4

Barclay, Col. A. T., 40

Barge, invention of, 210

Battleship turret, improver of, 95

Bavarians in the Tyrol (1809), 4

Beagle, H. M. S., Darwin's voyage in, 51

INDEX

INDEX

I N D E X

INDEX

INDEX

INDEX

I N D E X

Made in United States
North Haven, CT
26 February 2024

49254001R00192